Star*Date*Oracle  ™

Star*Date*Oracle ™

Sasha Fenton & Jonathan Dee

Zambezi Publishing

www.zampub.com

First published in 2001 by Zambezi Publishing
P.O. Box 221 Plymouth
Devon PL2 2YJ (UK)
Fax: +44 (0)1752 350 453
email: info@zampub.com   www.zampub.com

British Library Cataloguing in Publication Data:
A catalogue record for this book
is available from the British Library

ISBN 1-903065-15-1

Text illustrations by Jonathan Dee ©2001
Cover design: Jan Budkowski & Sasha Fenton ©2001

Printed & bound in Great Britain by:
Antony Rowe Ltd,
Bumper's Farm, Chippenham, Wiltshire
135798642

Star*Date*Oracle is a trade mark of Zambezi Publishing.

Sasha Fenton

Sasha was born in Bushey, near Watford in Hertfordshire, England. Many members of her family had an interest in psychic subjects. Sasha became interested in palmistry in childhood, and studied hands as a hobby for years before adding astrology and Tarot reading to her skills. By the time of her Saturn return at the age of 30, she was earning money as a consultant. It was the lack of accessible books on mind, body and spirit subjects that turned Sasha into an author in the 1980s.

A past Secretary and President of the British Astrological and Psychic Society (BAPS), Sasha has also held the post of Chair of the Advisory Panel on Astrological Education, and has been an active member of the Executive Council of the Writers' Guild of Great Britain.

Sasha and her husband, Jan Budkowski, live in Plymouth and publish books in the mind, body and spirit field, under the Zambezi Publishing label.

Books by Sasha Fenton

Sun Signs
Moon Signs
Rising Signs
The Planets
Understanding Astrology
How to Read Your Star Signs
Reading the Future
Astro-Guides 1995 to 2000 (with Jonathan Dee)
Living Palmistry (with Malcolm Wright)
The Book of Palmistry (with Malcolm Wright)
Fortune Telling by Tarot Cards
Fortune Telling by Tea Leaves
The Fortune Teller's Workbook
Tarot in Action!
SuperTarot
The Tarot
Body Reading
Dreams (with Jan Budkowski)
Astrology... on the Move!
Astrology for Living
Prophecy for Profit (with Jan Budkowski)
The Moon Sign Kit (with Jonathan Dee)
Astrology: East and West
Tarot
I Ching
Feng Shui for the Home
Introduction to Palmistry
The Book of Dreams
The Book of Spells
Tea Cup Reading
Chinese Divinations
Your Millennium Forecasts (with Jonathan Dee)
2001 Your Complete Forecast Guide (with Jonathan Dee)
Forecasts 2002 (with Jonathan Dee)

JONATHAN DEE

Based in Cardiff, Wales, Jonathan has been an astrologer, Tarot card reader and psychic since the 1970s, having traveled all over the UK and also in the USA. He is well known on radio, television and in a variety of magazines as a serious historian and mythologist in addition to his psychic skills. And yes, Jonathan is directly descended from the famous Dr. Jonathan Dee.

Jonathan has been the regular daily astrologer for BBC Radio Wales for the past 16 years, besides broadcasting on other radio and TV channels both as an astrologer and a historian. He has also presented a series of programs for BBC TV exploring the fascinating byways of the history of Wales.

As well as being a well-established author in his own right, Jonathan has often partnered Sasha Fenton in producing their annual Astro-Guide series between 1995 and 2000, the Moon Sign Kit and other titles. Jonathan has written on subjects as diverse as his illustrated guides to the Tarot, Runes, Feng Shui and Chinese Face Reading, as well as historical works on Ancient Egypt and the history of prophecies.

Books by Jonathan Dee

Astro-Guides 1995-2000 (with Sasha Fenton)
Tarot
The Chronicles of Ancient Egypt
The Book of Prophecies
Feng Shui
Feng Shui for the Garden
Feng Shui from Scratch
Tarot, an Illustrated Guide
Your Millennium Forecasts (with Sasha Fenton)
2001 - Your Complete Forecast Guide (with Sasha Fenton)
Runes, an Illustrated Guide
Chinese Face Reading
The Moon Sign Kit (with Sasha Fenton)
Forecasts 2002 (with Sasha Fenton)

Forthcoming titles:
Vampire Genesis - An Unnatural History of the Undead
Chinese Horoscopes
Celtic Runes
Color Therapy (with Lesley Taylor)

Dedication

To our special friends, Molly-Ann Fairley and Grant Griffiths

Acknowledgements

For all their help and guidance,
with grateful thanks to Glenys Ivans, Jean of Rainbow's End,
Bruce Cook, Apollonius,
and the spirit of Cagliostro

Contents

Introduction

This book contains three oracular systems, the first of which is the Star*Date*Oracle itself, followed by the List of Fates and finally the Mystic Pyramid.

Each of the three oracles works in a different way and has a different purpose. They are all based on ancient principles but all have been brought up to date so that they make sense in our modern world.

The Star*Date*Oracle ™

The Star*Date*Oracle takes just minutes to understand, yet this ancient astro-numerical system, refined, improved and updated by Sasha and Jonathan, gives you the power to make daily decisions that could change your life. You don't need special information, such the exact time or place of your birth, as is in the case with astrology; all that you need is your date of birth, to make this system work perfectly. You can use the Star*Date*Oracle to discover how a specific hour or a particular day will go, and it will even give you an overview of your life's direction.

You can use the Oracle in two ways, depending upon your circumstances at any moment in time. Firstly, you can choose a day on which you have something important planned to see what it will bring, and you can even refine this by looking at a particular hour of that day. And secondly, you can select the best hour within the best day for a specific action. You can even look back in time to see why something went well (or badly wrong) at some time in the past! In this way, the Star*Date*Oracle helps to put you in control of your own destiny, rather than leaving you to wallow at the whim of fate.

However, even with a system as carefully designed as this, we know that there is undoubtedly an element of generalization. After all, there are other people around who will share your Destiny Number or your major planetary influences. Although a personal consultation with a professional astrologer or numerologist is ideal, particularly if you have a vital decision to make, visits do take time to arrange and you may have to pay a hefty fee. The Star*Date*Oracle allows you the freedom to give yourself a reading wherever and whenever you like - every day, and even for every hour of a day. You will have the power to use and to choose your destiny at your fingertips and, ultimately, boost all your opportunities for success. Nevertheless, only you can decide to what extent you rely upon these oracles, and we wish to make clear that, as with any other systems of whatever kind, it would be unwise to pin important decisions on one source of inspiration alone.

Used with a good dose of common sense and in conjunction with whatever other data that may be available to you, these oracles can, but are not guaranteed to, provide you with very useful assistance in making all those various decisions we confront daily.

Use this book sensibly to get the most out of it, and remember that we cannot be responsible for your decisions - only you can.

The List of Fates

This is quite different from the Star*Date*Oracle, both in the way that it is worked out and also in the scale of the answers that it gives. Firstly, this is an alphabetic system that is worked out from the letters of your name; this being the name that you commonly use, e.g. Bill Smith rather than William George Smith, etc. The second difference is that the List of Fates doesn't confine itself to days, hours or other short periods of time, it gives an overview of your life and destiny as a whole.

The Mystic Pyramid

The Mystic Pyramid is different again, both in the way it is approached and in what it reveals. This is a numerical system that gives a list of questions for you to choose from and then 36 potential answers to each question. To find the right answer, you have to dowse over the Mystic Pyramid with a pendulum or a pendant necklace while concentrating on the question that you want answered. Then you consult the relevant list of answers to find the one that fits the Mystic number that your dowsing has given you.

Full instructions for all three systems accompany each of them, and little brainwork is required besides adding up a few numbers.

We hope that you find this book useful on an hourly, daily, short term and lifelong basis, both in the near future and through all the years ahead of you. You can consult this book at any time in order to look up answers for specific questions, to see how things are going, to help plan the best time for any enterprise and for advice and help in dealing with tricky situations.

We tend to use one gender (usually masculine) in our books, to ease readability. No slight or offense to womankind is intended.

Disclaimer

The British legal system tends to make it difficult for anyone to make money out of frivolous lawsuits - even if they find a solicitor to take such a thing on. In the USA - and perhaps elsewhere - things are different, so we have taken the advice of Dan Poynter, who has written an excellent book on publishing (The Self-Publishing Manual), and we have adapted his standard disclaimer for our own use.

This book is designed to provide information in regard to the subject matter covered. It is sold with the understanding that the publisher and authors are not thereby engaged in rendering legal, accounting, forecasting, financial or any other such services, of a professional nature or otherwise. If such assistance is required, the services of a professional should be sought. The reader's individual circumstances may require customised solutions for specific issues.

Information derived from this book should not be used as the sole or primary tool for making decisions of any nature whatsoever. As with any other tool or source of information, a large serving of common-sense is required, preferably with alternate supporting confirmation of an intended course of action. Readers are welcome to evaluate the contents of this book for themselves, and to make up their own minds as to what extent they may consider the contents of this book of use for their own purposes. Under no circumstances whatsoever can the publisher, authors, or anyone connected with the publication of this book be held responsible for any direct or indirect consequences deriving from the application of information contained in this book.

Using the Star*Date*Oracle ™

The system in this book is interactive, which in plain English means that you have to do something yourself before you can make it work. However, your part in the operation is extremely simple.

Your starting point for the Star*Date*Oracle is to find your own **Destiny Number** (*see this chapter*) by adding up all the numbers in your birthday according to the instructions.

Then you need to find the **Day Number** (*also in this chapter*) for the day you wish to examine.

Once you have both these numbers, you simply add them together, and if the total comes to more than a single-figure number, you reduce this again to a single digit - this is the **Prediction Number**, explained at the end of this chapter.

Armed with the Prediction Number, you can then choose to look up your prospects for today, tomorrow or any day in the future or the past. Full instructions and examples for all this are shown further on.

When you have discovered what your day of choice will bring you, you can then move to chapter 4, on finding the **Hour Number**, where you can look at a specific hour on a specific day and then see what it will bring. This means that, if you have an important event planned, you can pinpoint the planetary energies that will be at work at that particular time. Such an event might be life-changing, such as a wedding or a job interview, or it could be something quite mundane, such as meeting your partner for lunch, going to your child's school sports day or even treating yourself to a new pair of shoes.

We will show you how to choose or elect a time and day for a prospective event, to give it the best possible start, rather than simply drifting along, hoping that things will work out and allowing fate to be your ruler. This system not only ensures that the event itself will be a success, but that the long-term outlook will also be more favorable. A typical example would be sending an important letter or going out on a date - whether with a new acquaintance or with someone whom you see regularly. You may want to start some kind of small enterprise, or simply splash some paint around your bathroom. Even going to a hair salon or buying that special outfit needs the right influences and, goodness knows, a holiday can be a dream or a disaster if it is taken under a bad influence. Buying a home, getting married (or divorced) or buying a car are major events, but as life is made up of myriad small things, this book helps you to see the detail as well as the major turning points.

You can then discover the meaning of your **Destiny Number** and your **Power Planet** (*in chapter 4*), to discover the influences that will direct your life as a whole. Knowledge is power, so even if you don't like what life may be showing you, you can enhance the best aspects of your Destiny Number and your Power Planet to improve your outlook, to maximize your potential and to minimize pitfalls.

Finding your Destiny Number

According to the traditional rules of numerology, you take every number in your date of birth, add the numbers together and then reduce them to a final Destiny Number. So let us take 3 July 1990 as an example. The day is three and July is the seventh month, so it counts as seven, and the year is 1990.

Now add up every digit of the date: $3 + 7 + 1 + 9 + 9 + 0 = 29$.

Now add the 2 and 9 together: $2 + 9 = 11$.

And add the two numbers together once again, so that you end up with a single figure: $1 + 1 = 2$.

Therefore, the numerological value of 3 July 1990 is 2.

If you happen to be more accustomed to the American system of putting the month before the day, just add the numbers up in the way you are accustomed to, as the result will be exactly the same.

Here's another example. Jenny was born on 21 December 1975. December is the twelfth month, so it counts as 12.

Therefore, we add the digits of the date (21), the month (12) and the year (1975) all in one long row:
$2 + 1 + 1 + 2 + 1 + 9 + 7 + 5 = 28$.

Now add $2 + 8 = 10$.

Since zeros don't count in numerology, Jenny's Destiny Number is 1.

If Jenny were an American, she would express her date as December 21, 1975, and the result would be exactly the same.

The system can be used for Arabic, Hebrew, Chinese or any other type of number, as long as you end up with one digit that is nine or below.

Now follow the procedure to find your own **Destiny Number**. *(Note, too, that you can look up the meaning of your Destiny Number at the back of chapter 4 in the section on "Your Life Destiny", for a separate character analysis and life prediction).*

Finding the Prediction Number

Once you've found your Destiny Number, the rest is easy. Take any date you like, in any month of any year that is past, present or future, and repeat the process outlined above.

Let's say that you have a special event coming up; once you know the date of the event, you can reduce it to a single number in exactly the same way as you did when finding your Destiny Number. Once you have this new **Day Number**, simply add it to your **Destiny Number** to find the **Prediction Number**.

Now we can see how your fortunes will fare on that particular date. For instance, you may have 29 September 2001 in mind. This becomes 29 + 9 + 2 + 0 + 0 + 1, which boils down to 41.

Then add: 4 +1 = 5. The Day Number is 5.

Add this result to your own Destiny Number and voila, the numerology of the day as it relates to you, personally, is revealed as the **Prediction Number**.

Star Tip: *It's important to remember that if somebody else wants to look at their prospects for the same day as you, they must add their own Destiny Number to the Day Number in order to find their Prediction Number.*

Remember Jenny, our example, born on 21 December 1975? We worked out that her Destiny Number is 1. Now suppose she wanted to look up her fortunes on 13 April 2001. The numerology for that date is as follows:

April is the fourth month, so it counts as 4. So, the numbers of that date are added to Jenny's Destiny Number, and the sum is:
$1 + 3 + 4 + 2 + 0 + 0 + 1 = 11$.

Now add the two digits together, to find the single digit for the Day Number:
$1 + 1 = 2$. Thus the Day Number is 2.

All Jenny has to do now is to add her Destiny Number (which is 1) to the Day Number (which is 2) to arrive at a Prediction Number:
$1 + 2 = 3$.

This is all you need do for a daily reading. Later in this book, in chapter 4, we will show you how to discover your **Hour Number**. This helps you to fine-tune the system, showing you how to choose the best hour on a specific day for any event.

What Each Day Holds for You

From ancient times, the seven days of the week have been linked to the seven planets of traditional astrology. These are the Sun, Moon, Mars, Mercury, Jupiter, Venus and Saturn in that order. It's easy to spot Sunday as the day of the Sun, Monday as the Moon's day and Saturday as Saturn's day. However, in English-speaking countries, the other days are known by their Viking equivalents. Mars becomes Tue, the Norse god of war, hence Tue's day. Mercury was identified with the one-eyed Woden king of the Viking gods, hence Wednesday, or Woden's day. Thunderbolt-wielding Jupiter became the mighty hammer-swinging god, Thor, now surviving as Thursday. And Venus, goddess of love, was identified with the similarly amorous Freya, governing Friday.

Of course, in many European languages the link between the planets of astrology and the days of the week is even more obvious; for example, in French Tuesday is Mardi (Mars day), Wednesday is Mercredi (Mercury's day) and so on. According to this logic, it follows that each day has something of the influence of the planet that governs it. The cold outer planets, Uranus, Neptune and Pluto, were only discovered relatively recently, which is why they were not included in the original system.

How to Begin

Add your own **Destiny Number** to the **Day Number**, which gives you the **Prediction Number**, as outlined in chapter 2. Then take a look at the kind of energy that this Prediction Number contains, in the following pages.

Next, find the specific day of the week that the date of your Prediction Number falls on, and see what that will bring, by looking it up in the following pages.

If you want to check out a specific hour within a day as well, then turn to chapter 4, which deals with   the Hour Numbers.

Star Tip: Important notice!

We have discovered that those people who live in the Southern Hemisphere find that the Star*Date*Oracle is a day out of sequence, with events occurring a day earlier than they should. This also seems to apply to those who live at a distance from the UK, and it may be due to the fact that sunrise occurs at different times in different parts of the world.

Our advice to those in Southern Hemisphere countries is to test the system by trying out a few dates that have already passed by, and then read the Oracle for that day and also the days that preceded and succeeded it. You may (or may not) find a particular pattern emerging - for example, if your readings seem to fall a day behind, or in front of, those in the Oracle, adjust your future readings accordingly. It is too early for us to be more precise about this phenomenon at present, and we would welcome any feedback from "Southerners", for further development of the Oracle.

Prediction Number 1

A Number 1 energy brings opportunities for a fresh start. If you need to tackle something difficult, you will have the energy and optimism with which to do it. This is a good time to sign a contract, finalize an agreement or get started on a project. This is also a good day for chatting with interesting and intelligent people and getting some input and ideas from them. You won't be short of positive ideas, but you must analyze them to see if they will hold water. Avoid haste and impetuosity if you can.

If it is a Monday:

Number 1 is linked to the Sun, and Monday is linked to the New Moon.

This will be a day filled with good humor and pleasant company. Romantic dalliances will be very pleasing, but you may have a tendency to read more into statements than is actually meant. In most other areas of life your intuition will be on form and some of you will even experience a moment of psychic perception. Home and family life are emphasized under this influence, and your children may make you proud to be their parent. You may feel more like being around your family and loved ones than concentrating on your work. Your emotions might run a little high, either bringing you a touch of unnecessary depression, elation or even passion, due to the emotional effect of the Moon. If this day actually coincides with a New Moon up in the heavens, your urge to start something new will be enhanced; if there is a Full Moon today, those around you had better watch out, as your temper might be a little hard to control.

If it is a Tuesday:
Number 1 is linked to the Sun, and Tuesday is linked to Mars.

You'll be highly energetic and pretty courageous today. Your vitality will be on a high and you will be determined to get your own way - come what may! You may think that you are only standing up for what is right, but take care because you could come over as being rather pushy and aggressive. Your feelings will run quite high, but logic and common sense should prevent you from doing something really rash. If you have anything mechanical to fix, this is a good day on which to get such jobs done.

If it is a Wednesday:
Number 1 is linked to the Sun, and Wednesday is linked to Mercury.

You'll be thinking clearly and be able to express your ideas with a persuasive eloquence, and it is likely that you could charm the birds from the trees if you set your mind to it. You will be more attuned to mental pursuits rather than physical activities, although mending things or doing some kind of craftwork could be quite soothing for you. Those who like to look at recipe books or to cook interesting meals will be inspired. Today is favorable for all matters of business and negotiations, and for making others take notice of your views. Travel could also figure in your fortunes for the day.

If it is a Thursday:
Number 1 is linked to the Sun, and Thursday is linked to Jupiter.

You'll feel the need to assure yourself that past efforts have been recognized and suitably rewarded. You may become something of a social climber as you mingle with those from a different set today. Matters concerning travel, education and religion are well starred. This is not the time to take on board the opinions or beliefs of others unless they line up with your own. Belief in yourself will be the key to success.

If it is a Friday:
Number 1 is linked to the Sun, and Friday is linked to Venus.

There's no doubt that you are in a seductive mood today. Your powers of attraction must be working overtime, because you will turn heads wherever you go. It's a good thing that you are in a flirtatious mood, too, so you can make the most of this amorous influence. On a different level, if your self-esteem has taken a knock or two lately, today's events will help to even things up a little. This is no time to diminish your own sense of self-worth by focusing on your faults; we all have them, and yours are no worse than the next person's.

If it is a Saturday:
Number 1 is linked to the Sun, and Saturday is linked to Saturn.

This is a day for concentration. Whether you are involved in work or a hobby, whatever you are doing will require your total attention. Other people might think that you are being boring, but nothing could be further from the truth. In fact, you are accomplishing something that will stand the test of time. Anything that you start today should work out well in the end, as long as you remember to dot the "I's" and cross the "T's". Your mood will swing between happiness and slight depression, but by the end of the day you will feel satisfied with your progress.

If it is a Sunday:

Number 1 is linked to the Sun, and Sunday is also linked to the Sun, so this is a "double-Sun" day.

You should feel completely in harmony with yourself today. If you've been feeling downhearted or otherwise under the weather, then now is the turning point and you'll begin to feel more vibrant and confident. It is certain that romance, creative ventures and leisure activities will all go well. Business or money-making enterprises stand a good chance of success, too, especially if they are started now. Smile - sometimes it's good to be alive!

Prediction Number 2

This is a good day on which to continue a project and to consolidate what you have done so far. This is also an excellent time to mingle and co-operate with others, or to seek help from them if you need it. Partnership issues should go well, but sometimes a Number 2 day does bring conflict. Try to find time to relax a little during the course of the day if you can.

If it is a Monday:

Number 2 is linked to the New Moon and Monday is a Moon day, so this is a "double- Moon" day. This doesn't mean that there will be an actual New Moon today - although that is possible. If you look at the night sky and see a crescent that bends to the right, this is a New Moon, which will magnify the reading for this day.

Women will tend to do better than men today in all areas of life; one might say that the female of the species has the distinct advantage. There is a strong lunar feminine influence, so an indirect, subtle approach in your dealings with others will work best. Issues of motherhood and family matters will be to the fore, and these should turn out successfully for you. Domestic life will take precedence and, even if you are busy at work, you will be in a hurry to get home and cook a nice meal or to rush out and buy something for the home or for your family. Your emotions will be running in the fast lane today, so don't take any stray remarks to heart and, equally, don't force your own opinions on others.

If it is a Tuesday:

Number 2 is linked to the New Moon, and Tuesday is linked to Mars.

Emotions are likely to be highly charged today. It could be too easy to fly off the handle or to misunderstand an innocent comment and react to it like a ballistic missile. Take extra care; think before you react to anything because not all statements are a declaration of war. Whatever happened to diplomacy? The fur and feathers are most likely to fly in the home environment, so if your other half or your children get you down today, try to take a walk or leave the room and do something practical before you say something you will regret later. Having said all this, passions might run high in other ways and you could well end up - to quote John Lennon and Yoko Ono - making love rather than war.

If it is a Wednesday:

Number 2 is linked to the New Moon, and Wednesday is linked to Mercury.

The conscious and unconscious sides of the brain are in eloquent communication today, so logic and intuition will be your best friends. You'll be very perceptive and will soon have the opportunity to show off your wisdom. Short journeys and pleasant meetings with friends are likely. On a practical note, this is a good time to do something to improve your transport situation, so if your vehicle needs attention, get down to this now. This is also a good time to begin a course of study or training. Your mood is pretty good now and your level of confidence is high. Your emotions and your mentality are working in harmony, so you should be feeling pretty good about your progress in life, for the moment at least.

If it is a Thursday:

Number 2 is linked to the New Moon, and Thursday is linked to Jupiter.

This is a happy day on which you will be made to feel worthwhile. If you have to negotiate something important with people who are authority figures, this will go in your favor. In fact, it's a day on which you can win considerable advantages. An act of kindness will go a long way and it will come back to you in some beneficial manner at a later date. You mood may be slightly over-the-top with feelings of love or passion running away with you. Another possibility is that you fall in love with some new idea or concept and become convinced that this is the best thing since bubble-gum. You may be right, but a cold, hard look might show you that the idea has a few flaws in it. You will benefit from an unexpected stroke of luck now.

If it is a Friday:

Number 2 is linked to the New Moon, and Friday is linked to Venus.

Romance is in the air and a playful mood of amorous excitement is likely. However, if you aren't romantically attached, there's every chance that you will encounter someone who will become important in your life. You are sure to attract the right sort of attention from someone new at this time, and even if this turns out to be nothing more that a brief flirtation, it will be a nice boost to your ego. This is an excellent time to shop for bargains for the home and also to treat yourself to something new to wear. A good meal in the company of friends or loved ones will put a lovely seal on a great day. If you have something really magic in mind such as a second honeymoon, this would be an especially auspicious day for it.

If it is a Saturday:

Number 2 is linked to the New Moon, and Saturday is linked to Saturn.

You could be on your own for much of the day, but a little solitude is just what you need at the moment. There are chores to be done and it this seems the perfect opportunity to get down to them. This peaceful interlude will help you clarify your thoughts, and you'll get the satisfaction of a job well done at the end of it. There seems to be a need to look at life from a fresh perspective at the moment; a dose of reality can only be useful. You are keen to get on with some new phase of your life, but something from the past may need to be sorted out before you can do so.

If it is a Sunday:

Number 2 is linked to the New Moon, and Sunday is linked to the Sun.

Others will praise you and make a fuss of you today, and everybody will be happy to hear your ideas and opinions. Unexpected visits from friends and family are a possibility, and this would be all well and good except for the fact that your mind might be on more romantic pursuits. This is also a good day on which to start any sort of creative project, especially one that you either do at home or involves improving your home surroundings. If you find yourself on a first date with someone new the outlook is good, but it would be worth waiting at least a month before you decide that this is definitely the love of your life. Also, guard against selfishness or self-centeredness today.

Prediction Number 3

This is an excellent day for creative thinking and for coming up with problem-solving ideas. If you are into artistic matters, these will go well on Number 3 days. You should avoid behaving in an obstinate or irritable manner with others if you can, and if you need to stand up to others you should try to do this in a direct and assertive manner and not simply by digging in your heels. This should be a great day for parties, socializing and doing the things you like that don't necessarily include chores or work. If you need a meeting or a discussion, or if you need to take a short trip or to go shopping, this is a good day for such activities.

If it is a Monday:

Number 3 is linked to Jupiter, and Monday is linked to the Moon.

You'll be in an enthusiastic mood today and your popularity will be your most evident feature. You could also be generous with your time, money and expertise, and if your business involves you in any foreign dealings, you can expect good news from afar.

Dealings with women will be very beneficial, and this applies just as much to your friendships or family life as it does to business matters. Affairs of the heart should also prosper due to the lucky influences around you now. This is a good time to consider your beliefs and your motives and, if necessary, discuss your thoughts and needs with a family member. If you get on well with your mother or other female relatives, you will find them very easy to talk to, and they will be sympathetic and understanding towards you.

If it is a Tuesday:

Number 3 is linked to Jupiter, and Tuesday is linked to Mars.

Nothing and no one could possibly stop you today, even if what you are doing is basically wrong! You'll be extremely determined and convinced that whatever it is you are doing is absolutely the right thing to do. We're not saying that it isn't, but it just might be an idea to temper your forceful opinions. You feel lucky - and to be honest you may be right - but this is not an invitation for you to bet your shirt on the nearest horse race or expect to win the lottery, because your luck could come in a less material kind of way. Business and domestic issues will prosper today.

If it is a Wednesday:

Number 3 is linked to Jupiter, and Wednesday is linked to Mercury.

Your sound common sense gives you the edge today, and you could organize anything or anybody. If you have to use persuasion in negotiations, then you will be assured of a result that will surpass your expectations. Travel is also highlighted, making this an excellent day for journeys of all kinds. If you want, or indeed need, to take advantage of a training course or to improve your education in any way at all, this is an excellent day on which to make a start. If you simply decide to put your mind to some kind of knotty problem, you will be able to find the answer, and if you need to consult an expert, you will locate just the right person to advise you.

If it is a Thursday:

Number 3 is linked to Jupiter and so is Thursday, so this is a "double-Jupiter" day.

This is an extremely fortunate day, especially if you are involved in legal affairs, or dealing with contracts or travelling. Luck is with you in these matters and it will spill over into other areas of your life as well. You may be inclined to celebrate your successes a little excessively, but then it's not just any old day, is it? Jupiter is the largest of the planets, which means that on such a day anything that you want to improve on, to increase or to expand in any way will be successful for you. Your mood is somewhat philosophical and nothing will really bother you much one way or the other.

If it is a Friday:

Number 3 is linked to Jupiter, and Friday is linked to Venus.

Your social skills, outgoing, friendly nature and obvious charm will win friends and influence people today. The artistically inclined will do best, wining praise for their efforts. For those of a romantic nature, the amorous outlook is very good indeed. Who knows - Mr. or Miss Right (or even Mr. Right-Now) could turn up on this day. You will be in the mood to spend money, which is fine as long as you can spare it. If you can do so, then splash out on some new sports clothes or equipment, or book a holiday. Your mood is a happy one and little should upset you now.

If it is a Saturday:

Number 3 is linked to Jupiter, and Saturday is linked to Saturn.

It's a day for calm, concentration and perseverance. You are likely to have some big plans, but putting them into practice will take some effort, so your capacity for step-by-step progress is emphasized. You may need some peace and quiet to get on with things, but you will manage. Matters concerning property are well starred, and this is an excellent day for any business or career matters, because you can expect to be rewarded for past work and also gain immediate benefits from your current efforts, too. If you need the support of those in positions of authority, you will be able to rely on it now.

If it is a Sunday:

Number 3 is linked to Jupiter, and Sunday is linked to the Sun.

This is a day that should be filled with good humor and happiness. You will feel vital and alive, optimistic and outgoing. It's a good day for travel, socializing and indeed for doing anything that you enjoy. Co-operation is the keynote of this day, as you will find that those around you will help out in any way that they can. If you are interested in business, then this is an excellent day on which to start on something enterprising or expansive. You may try to take on a bit too much now, but your energy levels will meet the challenge and you will be able to cope.

Prediction Number 4

This is an excellent day on which to get jobs done in a practical and constructive manner. If you need to make a special effort or to attend to specific details, do it now. You should also reach out to all those who you have to deal with or co-operate with now, and also to pay attention to personal relationships and partnerships. The only problem is that you might ride a little roughshod over others in your haste to accomplish everything.

If it is a Monday:

Number 4 is linked to the Earth, and Monday is linked to the Moon.

Home and family life can be a joy, but then again, too much of a good thing can certainly take the shine off it on some days. Domestic duties will weigh heavily today and you'll strongly suspect that you are being taken for granted. You may also feel somewhat "nervy", or out of sorts. You need a break from routine but you can't have one just yet. If you can find time to sit down with a cup of coffee and a magazine or newspaper, just tune out for a while and indulge yourself.

If it is a Tuesday:

Number 4 is linked to the Earth, and Tuesday is linked to Mars.

If you meet any opposition today, your reaction (or should we say overreaction), will tend to be rather abrupt, or even aggressive. You may even take out your frustrations on someone who really doesn't deserve your wrath, so try counting to ten before you speak. On the other hand, it may be that you need to clear the air with someone who has offended you. Your mood will not be a particularly happy one, and all kinds of resentments will rise to the surface. This is not a great day for travel or for operating machinery either, as your concentration is not that good, so take care.

If it is a Wednesday:

Number 4 is linked to the Earth, and Wednesday is linked to Mercury.

You may be distracted today or even bored by someone else's incessant chatter. You could find yourself losing concentration in the middle of a conversation or talking at crossed purposes. It would be best to leave any important discussions or negotiations for a better day, because however reasonable your arguments, you will only meet with bloody-minded opposition. There's something on your mind and you can't seem to get to the bottom of it. Patience is the only answer at such a frustrating time.

If it is a Thursday:

Number 4 is linked to the Earth, and Thursday is linked to Jupiter.

An apparent stroke of good luck may not be all that it seems, so don't count on it too much. Good fortune may be delayed for a while, or the timing will be inconvenient in some way. An occurrence that you would usually welcome could arrive at the wrong moment, or when you are least able to deal with it. When your boat comes in, you're likely to be at the airport! As you can see, this is a difficult day and if you try to deal with others on a business basis you will only meet with rejection and opposition. Your gut feeling may be absolutely spot on, but it is absolutely no use trying to explain any of this to others - they just won't want to hear what you have to say.

If it is a Friday:
Number 4 is linked to the Earth, and Friday is linked to Venus.

The path of true love never yet ran totally smoothly, and today will prove that! Whatever you desire, you can be sure that your other half will want the opposite. A clash could be on the cards, but don't panic - this is probably just a minor hiccup in your relationship and it will soon pass. It's a great day to be single, though, as you can enjoy the company of the opposite sex for what it is without being expected to make a commitment. The only thing you do have on your side today is a great deal of common sense, so even if everyone around you is as daft as a brush, you will still be levelheaded.

If it is a Saturday:
Number 4 is linked to the Earth, and Saturday is linked to Saturn.

Keep yourself to yourself and don't expect too much in the way of co-operation from others today. Your best bet is to potter around the house and get some odd jobs done. If you are going to a special event then take care that you aren't indiscreet about some past peccadillo - and don't let anyone else's skeletons out of the cupboard, either. You are likely to feel lonely and at odds with those around you, or even profoundly depressed today. Try not to dwell on the black side of things, but just keep going, do what you have to do and then take a long, luxurious bath and have an early night. Tomorrow is another day and it might well be completely different.

If it is a Sunday:
Number 4 is linked to the Earth, and Sunday is linked to the Sun.

You will find yourself in opposition to those who are around you today. You may want to do one thing, but they will want to do something completely different. If you don't do anything at all, boredom will strike and you'll even get bored with being bored by the end of it. Don't sit around at home and mope: go out and find something to do. One thing that would be a success, and possibly a blessed relief, is to do some gardening if you can.

Prediction Number 5

"Five" days are particularly changeable, and indeed you may choose to change direction now and to try something new. However, this could just be one of those days when everything you had planned to do gets thrown out of the window due to unexpected interruptions or events. Short journeys or even longer trips could well be the order of the day. You could meet interesting people, or find yourself having new and different experiences. A 'phone call or a letter could take you by surprise.

If it is a Monday:

Number 5 is linked to Mercury, and Monday is linked to the Moon.

Both your conscious and unconscious minds will be in communication today and you will find yourself having almost psychic flashes of intuition. You may not actually be aware of this fact, but it will seem that answers to questions suddenly appear in your mind and you will be able to see through others with ease. Issues related to the different generations in your family or issues of motherhood come to the surface today, either in connection with you and a mother figure, or in connection with your children. If you haven't been in touch with the older members of your family for a while, this is the time to give them a ring. Finally, you could feel quite restless today and you may find yourself in a slightly edgy and depressed mood, which is hiding a great desire to escape in some way.

If it is a Tuesday:

Number 5 is linked to Mercury, and Tuesday is linked to Mars.

If you are faced with any opposition today, you will be able to argue your case forcefully and eloquently. Try to restrain an urge to shout or to lose your temper, because reasoned words will carry far more weight than any bullying techniques. Whatever the outcome, you can be sure that you will get your say. Vehicles could also play an important part in your life today, either because one needs to be repaired or because, at long last, you decide to replace one that is falling apart. If you habitually use public transport, you could well find yourself getting out and about on trains and buses.

If it is a Wednesday:

Number 5 is linked to Mercury, and Wednesday is also linked to Mercury, so this is a "double-Mercury" day.

You'll show yourself to be a complex individual today, being capable of developing many varied interests, and your curiosity will be endless. You'll be able to see the flaws in any argument and put up a devastating barrage of facts and figures that will put off any but the most determined opponent. You may be flirtatious or even fickle in your affections now, but everyone can play at the game of love once in a while, can't they? Your innermost need is for communication and understanding at this time and a good long chat on the phone to a sympathetic friend - especially one who has a great sense of humor - will do you the world of good.

If it is a Thursday:

Number 5 is linked to Mercury, and Thursday is linked to Jupiter.

You possess an uncanny ability to calm ruffled feathers today. Your powers of subtle persuasion and consummate diplomacy will win the day. In affairs of the heart, the romantic outlook is very good and there aren't many who could resist your charm and grace. Be careful with your credit cards, though, because you are liable to be a spendthrift. If you do go shopping, you are sure to come back with something other than what you went out for in the first place. Your mind will be working overtime at the moment, and you will want to read or watch television programs that make you think. It is unlikely that you will feel depressed and downhearted, but if you have reason to do so, try not to dwell on your problems.

If it is a Friday:
Number 5 is linked to Mercury, and Friday is linked to Venus.

Emotional desires could lead you astray today because temptation is all around you and you won't exactly be in the mood to resist. You may fall in love with a person, an idea or even an item for the home, but your fickle fortunes ensure that you'll soon have second thoughts. In short, don't commit yourself to anything at the moment. It seems that you have been bottling up a lot of feelings lately, and you may not have been able to find the right words with which to express them. Now is the time to open up to others and let them know what is going on in your mind and your heart. You may be surprised at how successful this is for you, but if your words meet a stone wall you will know where you stand and in its own way, this knowledge is valuable.

If it is a Saturday:
Number 5 is linked to Mercury, and Saturday is linked to Saturn.

A serious side to your nature comes to the fore now, and you will be capable of intense concentration. This is a good thing, because there are definitely some matters that need your undivided attention. Some wise advice could be coming your way, too, and you'd do well to heed the voice of experience. If you have any thinking to do now, don't just revisit your existing thoughts - analyze your position in life and see if you can come to some useful conclusions. On a more practical note, this is a wonderful day for doing those really boring chores and getting them out of the way. You will be rewarded with a nice, tidy house or garden, a sweet-smelling pile of ironing or your tax forms all neatly and correctly filled in.

If it is a Sunday:

Number 5 is linked to Mercury, and Sunday is linked to the Sun.

Your powers of persuasion will be very potent indeed today. Not only that, but your mind will be extremely active and it will be easy for you to assimilate complex information. The only thing to watch out for is that you may be rather opinionated and egotistical, which won't necessarily endear you to those you come into contact with. You won't be in the mood to sit around indoors, so take a shopping trip to one of those out-of-town malls or visit some kind of local event if you can. If you enjoy sports, this is the day to go out and enjoy yourself.

Prediction Number 6

Despite the fact that this number is often associated with quite hard work, there is evidence that you will be able to take some time off in order to do some of the nicer kind of shopping. By this we mean shopping for something other than food or other basic items. This is also a good day on which to listen to the music you like and to do things that make you happy, and it is also quite a good day for love and affairs of the heart. Nevertheless, work will take precedence during some part of the day and the chores will need to be done.

If it is a Monday:

Number 6 is linked to Venus, and Monday is linked to the Moon.

If your luck is in, this will be a quiet, rather domestic day - and that's just the way you'll want it. If you aren't so fortunate, your domestic bliss could be shattered by the demands of your loved ones who would like you to pay attention to them and their problems. To be honest, even if you are thoroughly interrupted by the needs of others, you will end up feeling quite good about it. Your emotions are on a fairly even keel at the moment and if you think about things for a while, you will realize that there is much for you to feel content about. Your female friends and relatives will be happy to come to your aid now and they will be even happier to join in whatever fun thing you have a mind to do.

If it is a Tuesday:

Number 6 is linked to Venus, and Tuesday is linked to Mars.

A sensual side to your nature comes to the fore on this most intimate of days. The passions will be stirred and those who are very fortunate can bask in an aura of love. This is an excellent time to show your partner how much you feel for him or her, and if you bring home a small gift in token of your affection, it will be very well received. Even if your amorous nature isn't stirred, it will still be a pleasant day filled with minor triumphs that should boost your ego. If you have anything to propose to others, you will be able to do this in such a nice way that they won't be able to resist your request. Even your work will be enjoyable and pleasant.

If it is a Wednesday:

Number 6 is linked to Venus, and Wednesday is linked to Mercury.

A message from an admirer is not unlikely today and you may even get a visit that will flatter you at the very least. Any new contacts that you make now could easily develop into a renewable acquaintance, so prepare to flirt and be flirted with. This should be a day notable for good humor, sociability and pleasant company. Words will come easily to you now, so if there is something you have been itching to say to a special person, get it off your chest. There may be some part of yourself that you find hard to understand, but a conversation with a trusted friend will soon open your eyes. It is unlikely that your friend will criticize you; on the contrary, he or she will be only too willing to point out your good side and to show you why others value your judgement so much.

If it is a Thursday:

Number 6 is linked to Venus, and Thursday is linked to Jupiter.

This is likely to be a very lucky day in all sorts of ways. You may have a small win from gambling or an encounter with someone who is destined to become important in your life. You may attend a celebration or embark on a happy journey of some kind. In short, anything you set out to do will be well starred today. Legal affairs should go smoothly and be very advantageous, as will any business negotiations. On a more emotional level, your mood is one of expansion as you simply can't be hemmed in and held back by others any more. If you have to say something about this to a friend or a colleague, your words will be surprisingly well received.

If it is a Friday:

Number 6 is linked to Venus and Friday is also linked to Venus, so this is a "double-Venus" day.

You'll be in an affectionate mood today. You will want to show your love in practical ways by showering your favorite person with gifts and tokens of your feelings. This is all well and good - as long as you don't push the boat out too far. Let moderation get a look-in because a bunch of flowers and a happy smile costs little, and often means so much more. You will not be in the mood for work at all, and any jobs that you try to do won't go well, probably due to a lack of any real interest on your part. If you can get off early and go out dancing or eating and drinking in good company, this will probably be better than doing things that you really aren't up to now.

If it is a Saturday:

Number 6 is linked to Venus, and Saturday is linked to Saturn.

You'll get the chance to show your loyalty to a friend or family member today. You will not shirk from taking on someone else's problems and even fighting for a worthy cause, if needs be. It may be that a troubled person needs a little emotional support; if this is the case then you are the right person for the job. There could be some extra money coming your way today, or you may start a new job or a new part of a current job that enhances your long-term prospects. People in positions of authority will be quite helpful now and if you have to use charm to get around bosses and so forth, you will be able to do so without any difficulty.

If it is a Sunday:

Number 6 is linked to Venus, and Sunday is linked to the Sun.

This is an excellent day for romantic dalliance and also leisure pursuits, so this is a time when you can indulge yourself without feeling guilty. We all need some time out, and this is your chance to get some. Of course, if you can share this with that special person, so much the better. Even if you are single, then you won't lack for pleasing company. Your self-esteem will receive a much-needed boost today and for once you won't have that nasty feeling that everyone else around you is cleverer, better looking or in some way more valuable than you are. Your creative talents will be quite obvious to others now, anyway. If you fancy indulging yourself in some nice toiletries, cosmetics or a new outfit, this is the right day for it. You will feel so much better for a bit of retail therapy.

Prediction Number 7

Matters concerning love, passion, affairs of the heart and relationships come to the fore now. Concentrate on your love relationships today if you can, even if it means neglecting some of your chores, because there will be something in your personal life that needs attention. This is also an excellent day on which to go on an inward journey and to do some thinking or to contemplate spiritual matters. If you have any studying or research to do, then this is the day for it. Try to use some part of this day for a little relaxation.

If it is a Monday:

Number 7 is linked to the Full Moon and Monday is also linked to the Moon, so this is a double-lunar day for you. This doesn't indicate that there will actually be a Full Moon in the sky today, but if you do happen to spot that the Moon is full, this will emphasize the importance of today's reading.

You are feeling rather sensitive today, because your emotional self could be quite vulnerable. Worse still, you will be able to sense the feelings of others quite strongly too, so if you are around negative, miserable people, their gloomy aura will tend to rub off on you. Cheerful people will help to raise the tide of your own feelings to a more pleasant level, so choose your companions with care today. It will be hard to accuse you of insensitivity now, because you will treat others with a great deal of care. Oddly enough, on a totally practical level, this is a terrific day for dealing with the public, or for dealing in goods that serve the public need in any way. Despite the Moon's usual association with home and family life, the world outside will be kinder to you than your own loved ones are likely to be.

If it is a Tuesday:

Number 7 is linked to the Full Moon, and Tuesday is linked to Mars.

You are likely to be rather volatile today, and negative feelings could come out to play if you don't keep them tightly under control. It's obvious that something or someone has upset your delicate equilibrium. Try to rise above unpleasantness and don't react by displaying anger, envy or resentment. Sometimes confrontations cannot be avoided, and they can even be useful in allowing you to state your case or clear the air in some way. This is all very well, but try to ensure that this doesn't end up in road rage or some other set-to with a complete stranger. Oddly enough, this is a pretty poor day for any sexual activity, as the passions aroused by lovemaking could actually end up in a fight. Stay calm if you can today.

If it is a Wednesday:

Number 7 is linked to the Full Moon, and Wednesday is linked to Mercury.

You'll be mentally active today with a line in devastating wit that will amuse, inform others and promote your personal interests. Your curiosity will be very marked now and you will find endless fascination in a wide variety of topics. Don't expect much peace, though - you'll be much in demand despite the fact that you already have plenty on your agenda and you certainly won't be bored. On a practical level, if there are letters you need to write or 'phone calls that have to be made, do all this today but do choose your words carefully - in what you actually say and what you put down on paper. If you allow your irritation to overspill, especially in matters of business, you could end up being sorry.

If it is a Thursday:

Number 7 is linked to the Full Moon, and Thursday is linked to Jupiter.

It's likely to be a happy-go-lucky sort of day when you can take a little time to enjoy yourself. Forget your duties for now and make the most of everything. Those who are travelling have a smooth path ahead, while those in business should make large profits. You will also be generous and supportive to all around you. Watch your emotions today though, because there is a feeling that you might go over the top in some way. For example, if you find yourself attracted to someone new, don't throw yourself at him or her too eagerly, but wait a while to see whether they are as interested in you as you are in them. Even a mild flirtation might come across too meaningfully, and you could end up feeling embarrassed by your own behavior.

If it is a Friday:

Number 7 is linked to the Full Moon, and Friday is linked to Venus.

There is a graceful, charming and artistic aura to this Friday. Your relationships will prosper, especially those that you have with women. Your home life will be happy and you are likely to make significant material gains. Your instinct for sniffing out bargains is at an all-time high now, so hit the shops today. All in all, this is likely to be a very lucky day notable for emotional contentment. The only blot on the landscape is that you might be feeling a little overemotional. This is all very well if you find yourself crying while watching a sad program on the television, but it could be embarrassing in other circumstances.

If it is a Saturday:

Number 7 is linked to the Full Moon, and Saturday is linked to Saturn.

A little self-restraint would not go amiss on a day when giving in to temptation will get you into trouble. Stick to the straight and narrow today because any deviation will be discovered - much to your embarrassment. If there are any difficult tasks to be done, you will possess the endurance and determination to see them through to a successful conclusion. You may find yourself in the center of a family dispute and it will be your job to pour oil on troubled waters, but you will have to accept the fact that you may not actually succeed in this endeavor. If those around you are in a belligerent mood, you may have to admit that even your silken words will do nothing to change their attitude.

If it is a Sunday:

Number 7 is linked to the Full Moon, and Sunday is linked to the Sun.

Although this is not an unpleasant day, your emotions seem to be out of tune with your rational mind. There is a sense that you are losing some objectivity, and possibly refusing to see an issue from another person's point of view. It may be that you are in the right, but it would be a good idea to examine your position once more just to be on the safe side. Even if your mind and heart are both in the right place, you may feel that others are simply not interested in your feelings or sensibilities. You may feel as though you are being tossed about by people in your family who belong to different generations, but who are so into themselves that they can't see your needs for looking.

Prediction Number 8

Financial and business matters rule when a Number 8 is in operation, so if you need to sort out your finances, pay bills and reconcile your check book, this is the time to do it. Business matters will flourish now, and if you need help or advice from those in positions of authority this is the time to ask for it. Also, you may be able to resolve a financial problem. Your intuition will be spot-on, so you can sit back, observe others for a while, and try to fathom out their underlying motives and agendas. On such a day, you might prefer to spend some time alone. One source of ancient wisdom says that if you are likely to hear of a death, it will be on a Number 8 day.

If it is a Monday:

Number 8 is linked to Saturn, and Monday is linked to the Moon.

You may wish to make an emotional declaration of some kind today - only to find that the opportunities to do so are somewhat limited. You may have to psyche yourself up to do something, and then find that your nerves waver at the last minute and hold you back. Perhaps this is not the best day to forge ahead, so be patient and bide your time. There is no doubt that you will be feeling a little blue right now, either because you have a good reason to feel downhearted or perhaps for no obvious reason at all. If you are simply rather bored and jaded with your life as it is at present, perhaps you can think of ways in which you can change things for the better.

If it is a Tuesday:

Number 8 is linked to Saturn, and Tuesday is linked to Mars.

This is not going to be an easy day, because your impatience will be matched by the frustration of not achieving the result you want. Even if you do gain your desire there will be something wrong with it, and you will end up dissatisfied. Nerves are frayed and tempers are close to the surface today, so take extra care. One good thing that you can do today is to work - the harder the better! So if there are any jobs that need to be done, this is an excellent day on which to get stuck in, and especially so if any of these tasks involve do-it-yourself or mechanical work. One really weird aspect of the day is that whatever the temperature of your surroundings, you will either feel too hot or too cold.

If it is a Wednesday:

Number 8 is linked to Saturn, and Wednesday is linked to Mercury.

Flippant remarks and flighty people will tend to irritate you today, because you have weighty matters on your mind and you will not want to be distracted. Serious issues should be addressed today because you will be in the right frame of mind to tackle complex or difficult concerns. There are times when you need to stop what you are doing and give some very deep thought to your situation in life, analyzing what is good, what is not so good and what you should be doing to change things for the better. If you take a kind of inward journey today and reflect on your current situation, you are sure to come up with a few sensible answers.

If it is a Thursday:

Number 8 is linked to Saturn, and Thursday is linked to Jupiter.

Two contrasting energies are present today: one is expansive and optimistic, while the other rather restricting and dutiful. You may have big ideas, but you know that a lot of hard work is required to bring them into being. You'll have no illusions about the mountain of tasks that await you, yet if you hold to your vision you will see things through to a successful conclusion. Business affairs are very well starred today as you can achieve a great deal without expanding your enterprise beyond what is reasonable. This may not be the best time to embark on anything new, but it is a great time to consolidate and to build on what you have achieved already.

If it is a Friday:

Number 8 is linked to Saturn, and Friday is linked to Venus.

It is hardly a day for social popularity, but you can achieve some marvelous things in your personal life all the same. If you were thinking of popping the question or committing to some long-term project, then this is the day to take your courage in your hands and go for it! If you have a partner, this is a time to be dutiful and supportive. Financial and career matters are particularly well starred at the moment so if you are trying to improve your prospects or your bank balance, the news should be good. If you need to talk to a parent, an older person or a person in some position of authority now, you will find it easy to do so.

If it is a Saturday:

Number 8 is linked to Saturn and so is Saturday, so this is a "double-Saturn" day.

You may be feeling rather out of sorts today, either as a result of past indulgence or just because you can't stir up much motivation. You won't want to be really bothered with company either, so some peace and quiet will be a much more attractive option. However, duty calls, so you must rise to the occasion. There is no use expecting to feel full of the joys of spring today, as you may be tired or simply extremely fed-up. You feel put-upon, misunderstood and out of step with everyone who is around you. There is nothing much you can do about this, so perhaps stick to your usual routine and then have a nice bubble bath and go to bed early with a warm drink and a good book.

If it is a Sunday:

Number 8 is linked to Saturn, and Sunday is linked to the Sun.

Today's outlook could go one of two ways, because either the events of the day inspire you to achieve great things, or they will make you think of all those things that you haven't done. This may be a spur to achievement or you could wallow in despondency. Pull yourself together and do something useful, because any enterprise that you make a start on now will go well in the long run. If you have the kind of goal in mind that requires a period of steady and sustained work, this is a good day on which to get on with that. Once you have broken the back of the task, you will feel so much better.

Prediction Number 9

This is a day for ending a cycle of events and generally completing jobs. You may want to look back on what you have achieved and make plans for the future, but you can't start anything new just yet. It would be best to avoid taking action or making specific decisions on a Number 9 day if at all possible. Just get those things out of the way that need to be finalized and get ready for the action to start again in a day or two. A specific piece of advice for this day is to be honest and fair in all your dealings with others.

If it is a Monday:

Number 9 is linked to Mars, and Monday is linked to the Moon.

Your nerves could well be on edge today and you may be feeling emotionally quite vulnerable. The unfortunate thing is that even a hint of a threat will meet with an aggressive reaction from you. You may be seeking to bolster your self-confidence with an expression of stubbornness or unreasonable behavior. Even if you start the day in a mood that is all sweetness and light, an older or younger member of your family is bound to set your teeth on edge before long. If you can use up some of your surplus energy or find an outlet for your pent-up feelings, then either vacuum the house from top to bottom or ask a friend to join you in a really fierce game of squash. Don't under any circumstances speak to your mother-in-law or anybody else whom you could easily upset or row with.

If it is a Tuesday:

Number 9 is linked to Mars and Tuesday is also linked to Mars, so this is a "double-Mars" day.

An action-packed, dynamic picture emerges as you show yourself to be energetic and determined. A forceful expression of your personality will ensure that you allow nothing to stand in your way, but this also means you won't be considering other people's feelings along the way. You'll overcome challenges with ease but you might make a few enemies while doing so. The best thing to do on such a day is to find a useful outlet for your energies, so if you have a difficult task to get done, this is the time for it. You must choose your tasks with care though, because detailed paperwork won't be for you now, although digging the garden, working on the car or doing any other physically demanding job will be just the thing. If you enjoy physical activity of any kind, such as sports or dancing, this is a great day for it.

If it is a Wednesday:

Number 9 is linked to Mars, and Wednesday is linked to Mercury.

You'll be rather impulsive today and ready to act at a moment's notice. Whatever pops into your mind will be put into effect immediately - with little or no thought about the consequences. On one hand, this should sort out a lot of the clutter in your life, but you must take care you aren't stirring up more problems for the future. Travel is quite well starred today, and if you have any jobs planned that involve a longish drive or if you want to visit friends who live at a distance from you, this is a good time to do so. You may need to say a few well-chosen words to someone who has been getting on your back, and today you are able to find just the right ones.

If it is a Thursday:
Number 9 is linked to Mars, and Thursday is linked to Jupiter.

This is a day for having fun - perhaps a shade too much fun, really. Today's planetary influences spur you towards overindulgence, and you won't be putting up much resistance. There could also be a tendency to gamble, take unwarranted chances or even risk your personal safety in some way. Slow down, and allow a little space for common sense. This is an excellent day for the start of just about anything, so if there is something that you want to get off the ground, this is the time to put some energy behind it. One rather strange quirk today is that you might feel inclined to force your beliefs and opinions on others, and this would not endear you to them. What works for you might not work for someone else, so leave them to their own beliefs and feelings.

If it is a Friday:
Number 9 is linked to Mars, and Friday is linked to Venus.

This is a day for intense feelings, but it is nonetheless enjoyable because most of these emotions will be pleasant. If you are married or have a partner, then this is a chance to re-ignite the flames of passion in your relationship. If you are single, this is the time to get out and about because the man or woman of your dreams could easily come waltzing into your life. Right now you should be looking and feeling better than usual. Even if what you see in the mirror is the same old you, other people will find you attractive. Dress yourself up and take yourself somewhere nice today, or persuade your other half to whisk you off to an interesting, attractive venue.

If it is a Saturday:
Number 9 is linked to Mars, and Saturday is linked to Saturn.

This will be an active day in its way, but you may not be able to concentrate on the things you had originally planned to do. In one sense this will be frustrating, yet in another sense worthwhile, because useful projects will be completed and you can take some comfort from this. This should be an excellent day for dealing with men, so whether you need to call in a plumber or talk things over with a male colleague, you should be able to get what you need out of them. Male family members will be on hand if you need any help today. This is a better day for practical achievements and getting ahead with the chores than for introspection or dealing with emotional matters.

If it is a Sunday:

Number 9 is linked to Mars, and Sunday is linked to the Sun.

This should be a very sexy day with your passions almost reaching boiling point. It would be nice to include love in this scenario but it isn't necessary going to be part of the scene today, because sex for the sake of it seems to be the order of the day. Oh well, a good horizontal workout never did anybody any harm, even if it is a little meaningless and unfeeling on this occasion. You may be seeking a mental challenge against which to pit your wits and energies. Today could mark the dawning of a very ambitious period, during which you will be determined to get to the top. Beware of overconfidence and too much risk-taking.

Star*Date*Oracle - Hours of the Day

The hourly Star*Date*Oracle lets you see what any hour on any day will bring. This hour number system has been around for many years, but although it is based on astrology, astrologers rarely use it. This system is far more familiar to pagans and those who are involved in witchcraft, because people who weave spells or perform rituals need to know which planetary god is ruling at the time of their rituals in order to gain maximum power for whatever it is that they are striving to invoke.

The Hourly Oracle is extremely easy to use. The table below shows every hour of the day in the left-hand column and the days of the week along the top. Track down and across to check which planet rules the particular hour on the specific day of the week that you are interested in. Then read the information pertaining to that planet to see what it will bring, and also what you can do to make the best of your special hour. If you add this third piece of information to what you already have for your Prediction Number and the day of the week for that Prediction Number, you should have a really good idea of what is likely to occur.

NB: In countries like Britain where British Summer Time or Daylight Saving is in operation during part of the year, jump back one hour during the summer months. This means that if you want to check out the hour of 20 to 21 (8 p.m. to 9 p.m.) and it happens to be BST or Daylight Savings, consider your hour to run from 19 to 20 (7 p.m. to 8 p.m.).

For ease of reference, the table below shows corresponding times for the 12-hour and 24-hour clocks from 1:00 p.m. until midnight. The Oracle as shown here uses the 24-hour system.

12 hr system	24 hr system
1:00 p.m.	13:00
2:00 p.m.	14:00
3:00 p.m.	15:00
4:00 p.m.	16:00
5:00 p.m.	17:00
6:00 p.m.	18:00
7:00 p.m.	19:00
8:00 p.m.	20:00
9:00 p.m.	21:00
10:00 p.m.	22:00
11:00 p.m.	23:00
12:00 p.m.	24:00

The Hourly Oracle - a.m.

HOUR	MONDAY	TUESDAY	WEDNESDAY	THURSDAY	FRIDAY	SATURDAY	SUNDAY
1	Moon	Mars	Mercury	Jupiter	Venus	Saturn	Sun
2	Saturn	Sun	Moon	Mars	Mercury	Jupiter	Venus
3	Jupiter	Venus	Saturn	Sun	Moon	Mars	Mercury
4	Mars	Mercury	Jupiter	Venus	Saturn	Sun	Moon
5	Sun	Moon	Mars	Mercury	Jupiter	Venus	Saturn
6	Venus	Saturn	Sun	Moon	Mars	Mercury	Jupiter
7	Mercury	Jupiter	Venus	Saturn	Sun	Moon	Mars
8	Moon	Mars	Mercury	Jupiter	Venus	Saturn	Sun
9	Saturn	Sun	Moon	Mars	Mercury	Jupiter	Venus
10	Jupiter	Venus	Saturn	Sun	Moon	Mars	Mercury
11	Mars	Mercury	Jupiter	Venus	Saturn	Sun	Moon
12	Sun	Moon	Mars	Mercury	Jupiter	Venus	Saturn

The Hourly Oracle - p.m.

HOUR	MONDAY	TUESDAY	WEDNESDAY	THURSDAY	FRIDAY	SATURDAY	SUNDAY
13	Jupiter	Venus	Saturn	Sun	Moon	Mars	Mercury
14	Mars	Mercury	Jupiter	Venus	Saturn	Sun	Moon
15	Sun	Moon	Mars	Mercury	Jupiter	Venus	Saturn
16	Venus	Saturn	Sun	Moon	Mars	Mercury	Jupiter
17	Mercury	Jupiter	Venus	Saturn	Sun	Moon	Mars
18	Moon	Mars	Mercury	Jupiter	Venus	Saturn	Sun
19	Saturn	Sun	Moon	Mars	Mercury	Jupiter	Venus
20	Jupiter	Venus	Saturn	Sun	Moon	Mars	Mercury
21	Mars	Mercury	Jupiter	Venus	Saturn	Sun	Moon
22	Sun	Moon	Mars	Mercury	Jupiter	Venus	Saturn
23	Venus	Saturn	Sun	Moon	Mars	Mercury	Jupiter
24	Mercury	Jupiter	Venus	Saturn	Sun	Moon	Mars

A Sun Hour

A joyful and successful hour

A Sun hour should be a happy and joyful one. Anything that you are considering setting out to do should have a great outcome if you start doing it during a Sun hour. A celebration that begins now should turn out to be a great success. If you are arranging a day or an evening in the company of someone you love, you will have a great time. This is a good hour in which to set off for a holiday or to treat yourself to something that you fancy. It is even a great time to make love.

Anything to do with children or young people will go well if started at this time, and even if you only spend time kicking a ball around with your children, you will thoroughly enjoy yourself. This is a great hour for success in business or in a social setting, and if you need to be the center of attention for some reason, there couldn't be a better time. The Sun's association with gold and jewelry makes this a terrific hour in which to buy a ring or any other sparkly token of love for yourself or for your partner. Business matters will also be successful during this phase. Remember that the Sun god, Apollo, loved music. Therefore, if you want to play music or go to a musical event or even to put on your favorite CD and relax for a while, this is a wonderful time for it. If you can do something that looks like being fun - even a game of Monopoly with the children - do it now.

A Moon Hour

An hour of sensitive feelings

There is good news and bad news connected to the Moon hour because this can be one of those times when your emotions will burst through whatever has been keeping them in check. There are occasions when you can put up with almost anything, but this is not one of them. Things that usually pass you by almost unnoticed will get you down now. If there happens to be a Full Moon or an eclipse occurring on this day, you will suffer from a form of premenstrual tension - and this will be the case even if you are too old for it or if you are a man!

On the other hand, this is a great hour for home and family concerns. Anything from a family gathering to talking around the dining table with your loved ones or simply relaxing in front of the television with your nearest and dearest will be great now. House moves, decorating, refurbishing, or anything else of that nature will go well if it is started during a Moon hour. If you want to contact older family members or spend time with them, there couldn't be a better hour. You may feel restless during this time, so try to arrange a trip out somewhere rather than getting down to work or doing chores.

Sometimes the Moon acts as a trigger to events, so if you are waiting for something to happen it should do so now. The influence of the Moon could make you quite perceptive and even psychic for a while.

A Mars Hour

An active hour

Mars is the action planet, so if there is something you need to do that requires action and activity, this is the time to go for it. There are a whole host of possible scenarios here but some ideas might include doing a tough, dirty or heavy job either at work or in the home or perhaps working on the car. If you need to make a mental or physical effort at work for any purpose, get started on this during a Mars hour.

If you need to state your case or to put your foot down this could be the time to do so, but remember that Mars was the Roman god of war, so stand up for yourself by all means but don't take things to the point where you start a real feud. Dealings with men will go well, and this applies to business matters or calling a builder or a workman to do something in your house. Passion in all its forms comes to the fore now, so lovemaking or passionate feelings will be reciprocated. If you are passionate about sports, you will be more energetic and competitive than usual and you could end up the winner in any game in which you participated during this hour. Even if you have a passion for something as innocuous as stamp collecting, you will find what you want and get where you want to be if you make the effort now. On a less pleasant note, you could find yourself at the dentist or undergoing some other kind of minor surgical procedure.

A Mercury Hour

A busy time with much contact with others

Mercury was the messenger of the Roman gods and he often had to do the dirty work for Jupiter and Apollo. You can expect to make a few 'phone calls and deal with correspondence during this hour but this doesn't mean that you will be expected to have to do someone's dirty work. It is simply a case of having to make contact with people and to communicate. You won't get much peace and quiet now, but you will manage to get a lot done.

There may be contact with brothers, sisters and neighbors at this time, and if you need help or co-operation from such people, this is a good time to ask for it. Mercury rules short journeys, so trips to the shops or errands of any kind will go well now. If you need to get a vehicle fixed, this is a good time to arrange it. Activities with young people and even indulging in gentle sport or other amusing activity will be good for you. You may be a bit rushed for a while, but you shouldn't be unhappy.

Mercury is associated with health and medical matters, so this would be a good hour to make a start on putting a niggling health problem right, whether by making an appointment to see a practitioner or by embarking on a course of treatment. Mercury was also adept at settling arguments, so tackle disputes at this time.

A Jupiter Hour

A time to expand your horizons

Jupiter was the king of the ancient gods and he could bring good or bad luck, depending upon his mood. As far as an hourly reading is concerned, there are a whole host of things that are worth doing during this period. Jupiter rules expansion of horizons, so you could book a trip or even arrange to travel at this time, and this is especially applicable to long-distance trips. Business that involves overseas customers, or even dealing with foreigners in your own land, will be successful during this hour. If you have any legal or official matters to cope with, this is a good time for it.

Jupiter rules education, so it's a good time to open your books and get down to studying, if this is applicable. Even if you only need to study how some new household appliance or computer program works, this is a good time to get your head around it. Jupiter rules belief and by extension religion, philosophy and spirituality, so if you intend to go to a Church meeting, a Spiritualist event, a psychic event or even to sit and think about what moves you, this is the hour for it.

Some see Jupiter as a lucky planet, and it is true that it is associated with gambling, especially horse racing. So if you intend to put a little wager on a horse or try your luck with the lottery, this is as good an hour for it as any. If the lottery is drawn during one of your Jupiter hours, this is even more likely to bring you luck.

A Venus Hour

Concentrate now on whatever is closest to your heart.

Venus is the Roman goddess of love, so it is easy to see what this hour is all about! If you are planning a romantic meeting with a lover or even with a potential mate, this is the time for it. Romantic evenings indoors are equally well starred. Obviously this becomes a good hour in which to get engaged or married, but it is an equally good time in which to start a business or some other money-making enterprise. If you want to buy something special for the home, try to do it during this hour, and if what you are considering buying is good to look at, so much the better.

Practical jobs of a creative nature will go well during this hour, so if you are into gardening, cooking or making attractive objects of any kind, this is the time in which to do it. Farming, working the land or even buying stock for a farm should all go well if started at this hour. If you are contemplating buying or improving a home, this is the time to start off the process. Money can be made from projects that are entered into now, especially if there is someone else who is also involved - although it would be wise to check out the Star*Date*Oracle for them as well as for yourself.

Venus is associated with beauty and luxury, so if you have money to spend on enhancing your appearance or on luxurious goods, this is the time to indulge yourself. This is a strongly sensual planet, so listening to music, looking at attractive goods or artistic things, or a visit to a pretty area, will do much to lift your spirits at this time.

A Saturn Hour

A time to attend to serious matters.

Saturn can be a hard taskmaster, so this is the best hour for getting difficult jobs done and dusted. If you need to talk to a boss or to someone in a position of authority, try to schedule this for a Saturn hour. Parents and other older people are more likely to be helpful to you at this time, although you will have to put yourself out or make an effort to contact them. This is a good hour in which to start a long-term project, to put down roots or to try to achieve stability in any sphere of your life.

You might feel weighed down with chores and you could feel tired, bored or irritable for a while, but the jobs simply won't wait and you must get them done now. Attend to details and make sure that everything you do is done to perfection, as sloppiness will be sure to catch you out now. You may have to work hard for a while but the results will be worth it, and you will be rewarded for your efforts. If you need to do anything that will raise your status in the eyes of others or give you a better position in life, this is the time to make it happen.

If you can't do anything practical at this time, concentrate on what you wish to achieve over the coming months. If you give some thought to your ambitions and your direction in life now, you will come up with a number of particularly useful ideas. Saturn is known as the teacher of the zodiac. While some of the experiences you may go through during this hour won't be particularly pleasant, you will gain from the experience, and the lessons that you learn now will stand you in good stead for the future.

Choosing a Special Date and Time

This chapter describes the influences behind each number and each planet, which makes for a far deeper reading than you could expect to find in any newspaper or magazine horoscope. This means that you can either read the Oracle sections (chapter 3) and leave things at that, or you can opt to search further by checking out the planetary section of this chapter and add this to the information that you have already been given. For instance, if your chosen day happens to be one that has the planet Mercury mentioned in it, you can look up the profile on Mercury in this chapter and add the information here to what you already have from the daily or hourly Oracles. Naturally, the same goes for all the other planets.

As far as the energies of the numbers are concerned, all you need to do is to review the information attached to each number in the Chapter 3.

Choosing the Right Day or Hour

You can use our Star*Date*Oracle to turn around the way you plan your life by choosing the right day - and even the right hour - for an important occasion. Thus, if you are planning a party or if you are making a date to meet a special person, you can choose to read the information here so that you can select the most auspicious day for your event. The same goes for an important business meeting, a holiday or any other outing that you have in mind. It doesn't matter what you want to do, the Star*Date*Oracle is here to help you.

Every Prediction Number and each planet contains its own special energy, so by choosing the right combination you can get the best out of your day. It would probably be too time-consuming (and perhaps even a touch neurotic) to do this every day, but it is definitely worth doing this for key events. All you need to do is to look through the information that we have gathered here and check out the energies of the numbers and planets to see which are most compatible with your plan.

Some Special Day Suggestions

The following list will give you a few suggestions about the combinations of numbers and a choice of the most useful planets for the purpose, but, as you can imagine, the list could be endless.

Event	Number(s)	Planet(s)
A wedding:	1	Sun or Venus
A holiday:	3	Sun or Venus
Buying a car:	5	Venus or Mercury
A job interview:	5	Saturn
A business meeting:	5	Saturn or Earth
A first date:	6	Venus or Mercury
A lover's meeting:	9	Mars or Venus
Throwing a party:	1 or 4	Sun
A quiet night in:	2 or 4	Moon
A tough job:	8 or 9	Mars or Saturn
Seeing your parents:	2 or 7	Moon or Saturn
Buying a house:	2 or 7	Moon or Venus
Decorating, refurbishing:	9	Moon
A children's party:	1	Sun
Buying something nice:	6	Venus
Giving gifts:	6	Sun or Venus
Picking a fight:	5 or 9	Mars or Venus
Cleaning the oven:	2 or 7	Moon

The Influence of the Planets

This section gives a full explanation of the energies of the planets, followed by a list of commonly known items that are ruled by each planet.

The Sun

The Sun rules creativity and bringing things into being. This doesn't only mean creating a masterpiece; it can be a home, a business, a garden or anything else that begins with an idea. Conceiving and rearing children, and the joy that they bring, is closely associated with the Sun. The Sun also rules success, achievement and personal glory. Some astrological systems also link the Sun to fathers and father figures, while others assign this to Saturn, the planet of authority figures and the older generation. The Roman god of the Sun is Apollo, who was also the god of music. These are perhaps the most important attributes of the Sun, but it is vital to bear in mind that the Sun rules your own actions and activities and the things you do, rather than the things that happen to you or that are done to you.

Quick List for the Sun
The personality and general outlook.

Creativity in all senses of the word.

Winning, succeeding, achieving.

Children.

Fathers or father figures.

Business, especially if it is successful or glamorous.

Show business, glamorous professions and life-styles.

Entertainment, holidays, amusements, games and to some extent gambling and games of chance.

Music.

Love affairs. These can be amusing diversions or deeply-felt affections, but they are supposed to be fun, even if they don't always feel like it at the time.

Organizing or taking charge - either in the sense of organizing your own day, or of rounding up others and motivating them.

The Moon

The Moon rules the way we feel, and this encompasses far more than our emotional life or our personal relationships. For instance, we may feel uneasy about something or we may feel in tune with something. The Sun acts but the Moon reacts and this intuitive, reactive response is often the right one. The Moon rules our habits and our behavior when ill, drunk or otherwise uninhibited, or when we are less mindful about what we are saying. The Moon represents our experiences of being mothered and it rules our actions in mothering others. It is also associated with the home and with the property or premises that we utilize.

The Moon rules domestic life, especially cooking and looking after the family. It can also mean providing the public with the things that it wants or needs. Thus, service to others and to one's own inner needs is enhanced at this time.

Quick List for the Moon

Inner feelings, emotions and emotional reactions.

Habitual behavior and how we are when we're less defensive, such as during illness or when we are drunk.

Mothers or mother figures.

The home, premises or property. The domestic scene. Also small shops or businesses that are run on a personal basis.

Women, female matters.

The public and supplying the public with what it needs.

Some health matters, especially chronic ailments or emotional issues.

Travel and restlessness.

Sailors and sewing and associated products or equipment, such as sails, nets, sacks and clothing.

The cooking and storage of food; thus the chef, larder, fridge, cooker, kitchen utensils; cows and milk.

Attachment to the past, patriotism, interest in history and collecting things that have a history to them, such as antiques or coins.

Mercury

The influence of Mercury is practical, mechanical and intellectual. It has nothing to do with emotions or feelings, but plenty to do with all those daily activities that we perform on a practical and unemotional level. Mercury rules thought, words, communication and knowledge. It is associated with local matters, travel and transport and the movement of goods and ideas. Negotiations, paperwork and education are ruled by Mercury. Mercury also denotes brothers, sisters and neighbors. Many of our normal, everyday tasks are associated with this planet.

Mercury also relates to work and service, either in terms of giving service to others, or by calling upon some kind of worker to do things for you. This kind of thing can relate to your job, or doing something, or calling someone else in to do something around your home.

Liaising with others, settling disputes and getting things down in black and white all come under the auspices of this planet. Theft and trickery are also associated with Mercury, so if you are out and about during a Mercury hour or day, be sure to stay alert. If you buy or sell anything, take extra care and ensure that you are happy with any agreements that you make, and that they are watertight.

Quick List for Mercury

Communications.

Travel and transport, also rail and bus termini.

Knowledge; primary and secondary education.

Local matters, the neighborhood.

The mind, mental processes, the way one thinks.

Brothers and sisters, cousins and similar relationships.

Youthfulness.

Health and healing.

Sales and marketing and negotiations of all kinds.

Thieves and theft.

Magic.

Venus

Venus, along with the Moon, is a feminine energy associated with the things that we hold dear to us. These include material possessions, land and also concepts such as our values and priorities. Venus rules sensuality and thus those activities and experiences that appeal to the senses: the appreciation of music, art, dancing, food, sex, fresh air and anything else that feels good and does us good. We can be very attached to the things we own or enjoy, and therefore Venus shows what we would fight to keep. This planet is also associated with relationships that are open to scrutiny. This could mean a love partnership or a business one, but it can just as easily concern an open and acknowledged enemy. Mars may represent the way we go to war, but Venus shows who we are fighting and why.

Quick List for Venus
Values and priorities.

Valuable goods, personal possessions and funds.

Leisure and pleasure, music, art and beauty.

Ostentation and luxury, decor and beauty.

Females.

Emotions that are connected to love and possessions.

Honest friendships and relationships, such as marriage.

Open enemies, reasons for fighting.

Mirrors, decorative glass, venetian blinds, (Venice is the city of Venus and the home of venetian blinds).

Cosmetics, powder compacts (with and without mirrors).

Sea shells, flowers, oysters.

Aphrodisiacs and venereal diseases (not AIDS).

Copper, malachite, emeralds.

Justice and fair play; legal arguments, arbitration.

Balance, harmony.

Mars

Mars, along with the Sun, is a masculine energy. It denotes passion, energy, competitiveness and drive, which can be used positively or negatively. On one hand, Mars adds assertiveness, courage and sexuality to a personality, but it can add aggression, violence and danger. Too much Mars is like too much adrenaline, but just the right amount gives you the heart to fight a necessary battle. Unlike Venus, this planet is not concerned with material possessions or objects, but its forceful energy may be the means of obtaining them.

Being such a masculine force, Mars is associated with traditional masculine pursuits and interests. Therefore, such things as engineering, do-it-yourself jobs that involve the use of tools, and anything that requires the use of heat, fire or energy come under the rulership of Mars. Anything that needs to be done quickly can be tackled now.

Competitive sports, whether these are team games or individual competitions, belong to this planet, which makes a Mars hour or day a good time to compete and to win.

Quick List for Mars

Energy, assertiveness, forcefulness, initiative.

Passion; the desire for something.

Decision-making, decisive action.

Arguments and violence.

Dealing with the police or armed forces.

Traditionally masculine occupations such as engineering, mechanics, steel making.

Competitive activities, especially sports.

Iron and steel, surgical instruments. Tools, especially knives, blades, chisels, screwdrivers and so forth.

Warfare, weapons, the tools of destruction.

Blood.

Jupiter

Jupiter signifies expansion and exploration, so anything that pushes back boundaries, surmounts barriers or creates opportunities is ruled by this planet. There are some traditional areas of interest that are associated with this planet, which you will find outlined on the following page. However, the general feeling is that anything that stretches the mind, increases one's experience or that leads to more understanding for oneself, or that opens the minds of others, belongs to the realm of Jupiter. Therefore, such things as higher education, long distance travel and exploration, delving into spiritual matters and belief systems or testing the law come under this influence.

Strokes of luck, especially connected with gambling and horse racing, are ruled by Jupiter. Nevertheless, in a more general sense, Jupiter encourages us to spot a small window of opportunity and to make something much larger out of it.

A Jupiter influence can start out by being destructive - after all, this was the god who threw down thunderbolts when he was dissatisfied. However, whatever is destroyed or brushed out of the way always makes way for something that follows, which is bigger and better than what went before.

Quick List for Jupiter

Foreign travel or exploration of new places.

The law and the legal system.

Belief, religion and philosophy; strong moral (or immoral) interests.

Education, especially higher education.

Money, business and success.

Opportunities, new and influential people.

Publishing and broadcasting.

Large animals, outdoor life and sporting activities.

Gambling and winning (traditionally horse racing).

Saturn

Saturn is often blamed for all our ills, especially by those who are new to astrology, but this is unfair. Saturn may be a hard taskmaster but he gives us the opportunity to learn and ultimately to develop character and backbone. Saturn is about reaching goals and picking up rewards for our efforts. Limitations, heavy responsibilities, difficult circumstances and times of restriction are seen here but they are part of all our lives at some point or other. This planet presides over craftsmanship, attention to detail and ultimate success through hard work.

Saturn is concerned with status, position and authority, and in more ancient forms of astrology, also with old age. This can indicate that during a particular day or hour, you will need to act with maturity and exert authority over others; the alternative is that you will find yourself having to cope with authority figures yourself for some specific purpose.

Saturnian authority can be the type that you as a parent need to exert over your children from time to time, but it can also mean coming across a person who lectures you, or treats you like a child. There is a fine line here between parental guidance and the kind of sensible instructions that an expert or person in authority would give you on the one hand, and tyranny on the other.

Quick List for Saturn

Endurance, persistence, restraint, caution.

Self-discipline, organization, sense of timing.

Ambition, success that is deserved.

Maturity, senior citizenship, old age.

Some aspects of pain and suffering, especially chronic ailments.

Banking, big business, corporations.

Structure and firm foundations.

Authority and status.

Lead, pipes, plumbing and plumbers.

Clocks, watches and timepieces. Time itself.

Masonry, building materials, the building trade.

Taboos.

Your Life Destiny

You will have found your Destiny Number when you added together all the numbers in your date of birth. The following section will give you a brief insight into the kind of psychology and life path for each Destiny Number. You will notice that in addition to the numbers that run from 1 to 9 that we use in the Star*Date*Oracle section of this book, we now also take a look at the double numbers of 11, 22 and 33. If your birth date adds up to one of these numbers, you would have to reduce it to a single number for the predictive readings in this book, but in this section you can also read the special numbers 11, 22 and 33 in their own right.

Your Destiny Number is 1

You may have been dominated and bullied as a child. One or both of your parents had the conviction that they were always right, possibly due to their religious beliefs, and pressure was put upon you to perform or to conform to their ideal. The upside of this is that you will turn out to be a hardworking and ambitious person, especially suited to self-employment or to reaching the top in your profession. The downside is that you yourself may copy your parent's pattern and seek to dominate others in your turn. Alternatively, you may become anxious and fearful of the future. If you find someone who loves you and who gives you the emotional support and understanding that you need, you will overcome all this. You could well become a success story in your career while also being valued for your honesty, generosity, sense of humor and adventure.

Your Destiny Number is 2

There may have been considerable tensions in your family background that may lead to you developing a hard shell in order to protect your vulnerability. Childhood events may give you the kind of insecurity that you relieve by becoming penny-pinching and miserly. You may seek to acquire goods in order to make yourself feel safe. Even if you don't go to this extreme, you will probably always be careful with money and possessions but in a reasonable manner. You are very keen on family life and you will be fiercely loyal to your family, loved ones and even to employers. You are not a natural leader, because you prefer to help others and to be appreciated for what you do for them. You may choose to work in one of the caring professions.

Your Destiny Number is 3

Yours is a very creative number, so you may be quite artistic or have literary talents, which you may not have been encouraged to express this during your youth, leading to frustration. You probably found it difficult to stand up to your parents and you may have a problem with authority figures throughout your life. This may mean that you can be stubborn and irritable in your dealings with others, or too charming and accommodating. Despite a difficult start, you usually do well in your chosen profession and you can be extremely lucky in your choice of friends and colleagues who help you where they can. You are sociable, flirtatious and you enjoy having a good time and seeing others enjoy themselves, too.

Your Destiny Number is 4

Your childhood should have been a happy one with plenty of love and support from your family and teachers. This may encourage you to lean on others later in life, treating them as replacement parents or teachers. You will always be a hard and reliable worker with a sensible attitude to whatever you take on. You are loyal and sensitive to those you love and you are also a loyal employee, although you can also succeed in a business of your own. You may be a little unimaginative, but you make an excellent financial advisor or craftsman, and your capacity for hard work will earn you rewards. You are a loyal and loving family person.

Your Destiny Number is 5

Your parents were reasonable and your childhood fairly happy, but there were events that made you feel very insecure. Your parents may have moved around a lot and you could have gone through several changes of home and/or school, or there may have been some health problems. You may tend to walk away from problems rather than face them. Your desire for the admiration of others may lead you to success in sports or the media. You are clever and versatile, and you need variety in your life and a number of different challenges in your job. You also need to travel around and meet a variety of different people in your working life and social life. You accept the ideas of others and you can be a good leader, allowing others to do their jobs without undue interference. You cannot have a relationship with a boring partner.

Your Destiny Number is 6

You felt extremely insecure when young and you may have had parents who either didn't communicate or who gave you strangely mixed messages. Your mother may have had some sensible things to say but also some very fixed ideas that were not normal or logical. Your family would have venerated hard work and you may have sought to impress them and to win their approval by working hard even as a child. The outcome is that you become a tireless worker in adult life, wearing yourself out for the sake of others. If your family or your employers appreciate and value you for the efforts you make, you feel that you have achieved all that you have set out to do. Your chief fault is that you may be too much of a perfectionist. Your mind is excellent and you do much to help others, often through a genuine desire to make the world a better place.

Your Destiny Number is 7

You probably had a fairly easygoing relationship with parents and other adults, partly because you are reasonable, sociable and pleasant. You can turn your amiable nature to your advantage both in your career and in personal relationships later in life, but you will need to guard against a tendency to let opportunities pass you by. You must avoid sitting back and allowing others to make progress at your expense or to take what should rightfully be yours. You prefer thinking to acting; you also tend to sit back and observe the world and all that goes in it. You may become a philosopher, a mystic or an artist. You are extremely wise but you may not use your talents or wisdom to achieve much. If you can develop your artistic talents and also find a stronger or more practical life partner, you will discover just how much the world appreciates you.

Your Destiny Number is 8

Your childhood will not have been easy, either because you were rebellious and disinclined to conform, or because one or both of your parents was domineering, dictatorial or rigid. You may have dealt with this by defying your parents or by using cunning and sly behavior to get what you wanted despite them. Either way, you learn to use charm later in life to get what you want. You are extremely intuitive and you can sum up people and situations almost in a flash. Add this to your sharp intelligence, your organizational ability and your capacity for hard work, and it is easy to see that you will make a tremendous success of your chosen career. You are the one who will end up with wealth and status. You may become domineering yourself in later life and you may see even your personal relationships as a kind of power struggle. If you can curb your sharp tongue and learn to be tolerant of those who aren't lucky enough to be born with your strength and courage, you can make your loved ones happy and in turn become happy yourself. You need to ease up a little and learn to relax and enjoy life.

Your Destiny Number is 9

Your parents were keen for you to do well and you could go on to prove them right by becoming a success. You have an inner urge for exploration, and this could take you into the realms of education or hobbies and interests that give you an opportunity to look at things from a variety of different angles. In many cases, the visionary aspect of your nature leads you to get involved in religion, philosophy or the spiritual life and you can also inspire others. Travel is a strong theme in your life, and you could end up seeing a fair bit of the world. You use your ability to get on with all manner of people to bring you success in business, but there is a side of your nature that could lead you to simply drift along without getting anywhere very much.

Your Destiny Number is 11

Your childhood might have been reasonable, but something made you determined to keep yourself to yourself. You may have been distrustful of adults or of other children or disinclined to listen to anything that others had to say. You seem to have been a quiet and rather serious child. In later life, you could become opinionated, inflexible and difficult. You may develop a terrific inferiority complex, which you may then cover up with an arrogant, uncaring or defiant attitude. If you find the right career outlet for your talents and develop sensitivity towards others, you may overcome your natural tendency for self-absorption. You have an original mind and you are attracted to unconventional ideas and an unconventional lifestyle. Marriage, children and a routine family life might never appeal to you.

Your Destiny Number is 22

You either loved and admired your parents, or feared their strength and domination. You grow up to become an independent person with an unusual outlook or nonconformist attitude. You understand the underlying motives of others. You also have an uncanny feel for the structure of materials and this could lead you to become a builder, civil engineer, architect or creative artist. You also make an excellent counselor and guide to younger people. If you can control your tendency towards angry or wounding outbursts, you can succeed in a relationship, especially one with a partner who needs to be guided and cared for.

Your Destiny Number is 33

You may have been somewhat isolated during your childhood, possibly due to illness and spells in hospital. This leads you to develop your creativity and imagination. Later in life when storms threaten, you can escape into a dream world of your own making. Your parents were not particularly hard on you, but life and circumstances have made you a little fearful. You will probably end up in one of the caring professions. You might take up spiritual work where you spend your life helping and giving yourself to others. The danger here is that you become overtaken by the needs of others and that you expend your energies, which makes you feel drained and exhausted. If necessary, you can be practical and also very successful, but you probably will always want to help others. If you can develop your artistic talents and work quietly on your own projects, you can achieve considerable success.

The List of Fates

An ancient system for working out the destiny hidden in your name

Quite apart from the significance of the personal destiny numbers to an individual's character and fate, the arts of numerology have taken many other forms in their long history. One of these forms was called the Cabalistic Oracle or List of Fates.

Some have claimed that this type of number divination is very ancient indeed going back to the ancient Greek sage Pythagoras who taught that the entire universe was governed by the power of numbers, to each of which he ascribed mysterious properties and virtues. Other authorities have maintained that this calculation is based not on Greek philosophy but on that of the ancient Hebrews, most especially on the secret knowledge that Moses brought out of Egypt at the time of the Exodus.

The question of origin aside, the List of Fates is based on the letters of the alphabet. Each letter is ascribed a numerical value from 1 to 1,400 and does not require any special skills other than the ability to add up.

The letters and their number equivalents are as follows:

A	=	1	N =	40
B	=	2	O =	50
C	=	3	P =	60
D	=	4	Q =	70
E	=	5	R =	80
F	=	6	S =	90
G	=	7	T =	100
H	=	8	U =	200
I	=	9	V =	700
J	=	600	W =	1,400
K	=	10	X =	300
L	=	20	Y =	400
M	=	30	Z =	500

At first glance, it might seem strange that the letter J is ascribed a value of 600, coming as it does between 9 and 10. This is because in the original order of the letters according to this system, J came at the end of the alphabet, following Z. Equally, later versions of the system include the previously missing W and give it a value of 1,400 because, originally, this letter was considered to be nothing more than two V's placed side by side. Since each V counts as 700, the final sum remains the same.

Character and Fate

The first step of the List of Fates is to write down the name of the person whose essential character and course of fate you wish to learn. It is advisable that you use the most commonly used name. Research has shown that very few people go through life with the name that is on their birth certificate. Even now, many women marry and change their names, while others change their names for a variety of reasons, or they commonly use a middle name or a shortened version of their original name. So if someone is generally called Liz instead of

Elizabeth, Bill instead of William, or a completely different name to that which is on their birth certificate, this "common" name is the one you use. Once you have noted down the person's name, jot down the number equivalents for each of the letters.

When you have added all the name numbers, it is possible that the final sum of the numbers will come to more than 1,300, which is the highest number in the list of fates. If this does happen, then cut off the first (left-hand) figure and only use the remainder. It is also possible that the interpretations of character derived from the List of Fates may appear to be contradictory in some cases. However, remember that, as we all know, some people are often a mass of contradictions. It is in reconciling these opposites that their true inner nature can be found.

Example 1.

If the name to be examined is Liz Hughes, the calculation is as follows:

L = 20, I = 9, Z = 500, H = 8, U = 200, G = 7, H = 8, E = 5, S = 90. Added up, the final sum is 847.

L	20
I	9
Z	500
H	8
U	200
G	7
H	8
E	5
S	90
	847

Having arrived at the final figure, it is time to consult the List of Fates. This might not be completely straightforward, because the final figure is unlikely to appear on the list, although its parts will. If we return to our example of Liz Hughes, her final sum was 847, and this number is not in the List of Fates. However, the component parts of this number *do* appear, which means that Liz could look up the numbers 8, 4, 7, 40, 47 and 800. The numbers 47 and 840 don't appear in the lists, but any such component numbers that do appear in the List would be valid. This uses all the numbers in the total sum but still keeps them in the order in which they appeared (i.e. from left to right, so that 48 and 74 would not be valid in this example).

In short, use all component numbers that can be extracted from the total number, just keep them in the original order; no reversals are allowed.

If you were to look up each of these numbers, you would discover that Liz has many different sides to her personality. Such variations would be found on an astrological chart, the lines on Liz's hands or any other kind of character reading; we do all have many sides to our personalities.

Example 2
Now let us take a well-known celebrity as an example, and in this case it is someone who changed his name completely This man was born with the name Issur Danielovitch and he has publicly said that if he had chosen to be a ballet dancer, he probably would have stayed with his original name, but in fact he became a very well-loved film star known as Kirk Douglas - father of film star Michael Douglas:

K	10
I	9
R	80
K	10
D	4
O	50
U	200
G	7
L	20
A	1
S	90
	481

We chose these examples at random, one being an unknown person who works in the media, and the other being an international star, but look how similar their component numbers are! Clearly these two people have similarities in their natures and in their chosen careers, but the difference in the layout and the transposition of the highly self-motivated number 1 for the more spiritual and escapist number 7 makes a world of difference.

In Kirk Douglas's case, he would need to look at the numbers 4, 8, 1, 48, 80, 81 and 400, because this covers all the numbers while still keeping them in their right order. We can, for example, use 81 here, but not 18.

It is also interesting that the number 81 is the only number in the 80 to 90 group. As you can see, the quantity of component numbers and the "special" nature of the 81 show just what a complex and interesting character we are dealing with here.

The List of Fates

1.   This number denotes a passionate and fiery personality, one who is ambitious and who will overcome all manner of obstacles to achieve them. The forceful nature of this fate number is obviously related to the energies of the Sun. It is direct, possibly arrogant and extremely determined. There are no ambiguities in this person.

2.   This is an unhappy fate showing much personal loss and grief. However this person will find the inner strength to cope with these misfortunes. The number 2 is governed by an eclipse of the moon. The one good thing to say about this number is that if it is part of a person's fate then he or she will achieve great wisdom.

3.   This is an extremely philosophical number governed by the planet Jupiter. Those with 3 as a fate number are deep thinkers who are interested in all aspects of belief. It may denote a strong religious or ethical sense. The number also promotes good fortune and 3 type people will travel far, either physically or in the spiritual sense.

4.   Solid, practical and extremely dependable, people who have 4 as part of their fate partake of the nature of Earth. Likewise, they are wise, realistic, home loving and are likely to be blessed with many accomplishments through dint of hard work. They may take their time but you can be sure that they will get there in the end.

5.   This number has associations with dexterity and the use of intelligence. The number 5 is governed by the planet Mercury. People with 5 as a fate number are often found in the

caring professions but they may equally be skilled workers, persuasive salesmen, writers, public speakers or broadcasters. They generally "live on their nerves".

6.   This number denotes perfectionism. This fate is connected with achieving something worthwhile and creating something completely new. The number is governed by Venus meaning that relationships, a sense of style, good taste and indeed, the good life are all very important to a person with 6 as a part of their fate.

7.   A love of freedom and the escape from restrictions is the fate shown by 7. This person will achieve perfect happiness. This number is also a sign of remarkable progress. The number 7 is governed by the full moon and those who have it as part of their fate will be very protective, caring and possibly psychic.

8.   A powerful sense of right is the fate shown by this number. Its main attribution is justice so this character will seek balance and rightness in everything he does. Saturn governs the number, so someone influenced by 8 will be rather hard on himself, and may feel isolated and insecure, even though he is extremely capable.

9.   Nothing is quite right or good enough for a person whose fate is influenced by 9. Disappointments, personal and financial losses are likely. The aggressive number 9 is governed by Mars, but the impulsiveness of this planet must be strictly controlled if the unfortunate implications of 9 as a fate number are to be avoided.

10.   This number suggests a clear and rational mind. This person will know great highs and lows in life but nevertheless his progress will be onward and upward. The greatest successes will be achieved in later life. The declining years will be notable for their contentment and comfort.

11.   This person must learn to admit his faults and make amends for wrongdoing. This could show a difficult and aggressive character always ready for a confrontation and usually finding one. However it is possible that with effort and dedication that all this wasted energy can be directed into worthwhile activities leading to personal success.

12.   This number shows good fortune and reveals a character who is a good-natured, sophisticated lover of novelty. His best chance of fortune will occur if he lives in a large city or possibly several large cities in turn because this number is associated with international connections and foreign travel. This is a person with wide horizons.

13.   The dreaded 13 reveals a marked degree of cynicism, mockery and repressed anger. He is likely to have been terribly deceived in early life or had an unfortunate upbringing. This person is not likely to believe in anything of a spiritual nature and inclined to trust nothing that cannot be proven by the physical senses.

14.   Persons with the number 14 as part of their fate are likely to have to make many sacrifices to gain their desires. This can be thought of as a "karmic" number, expressing the idea that in this lifetime is one of paying off debts incurred in previous existences. The concept of purification is central to this philosophy.

15.   The physical body is important to a person with 15 as a fate
number. He may be vain and anxious to improve the phy-
sique or at least the appearance of the physical form. In many
ways, it could be said that a 15 type person believes in the
Greek ideal of the perfect mind in the perfect body... in theory
at least.

16.   This character is very sexy with an alluring personality and
also very probably good looks. At best it shows a perfect
lover, at worst a callous seducer. On the other hand, no one
seems to complain too much about this person's amorous at-
tentions, unless of course the person's spouse is the jealous
type. A string of relationships is not unlikely.

17.   It is said that those who forget the past will inevitably relive
it, and that is certainly the case with the 17 type person. This
type rarely learns from past mistakes and will reject helpful
advice out of hand. It is unfortunate that this situation will
not change until he can accept that an error has been made in
the first place.

18.   A person with the number 18 prominent in his fate is likely
to have had a rough ride and known the cruelty of others.
Although this has toughened the character it also hints at a
kind heart which has been concealed for reasons of self-pres-
ervation. He may appear to be a tough cookie but is a softie
inside.

19.   Although a person with 19 prominent among the fate numbers may be clever he will be inclined to have monumental
"blind spots" and make the most grievous mistakes. It would
be kindest to say that this person is inclined to folly, unwise

associations and also would be well advised to steer away from financial speculation.

20. This number (like its base number 2) is rather unfortunate and may point to poverty, sadness and depression. The start of life may have been sad but that is no reason to allow such misfortune to ruin the entire existence. A break with the past and considerable courage are required for this person to achieve all potentials.

21. A person who is influenced by the number 21 usually likes to be something of a mystery. This one is self-protective and thus difficult to get to know. Issues of trust may be problematic so a potential friend or lover will need to be subtle and persistent to get anywhere. The 21 type person is deep, perceptive and intelligent.

22. Traditionally, 22 was regarded as a number of perfection; however life isn't too perfect, so a person who is influenced by this number will put a lot of effort into improving things. He or she might also be prone to "victim consciousness", imagining that if left to itself, life will invariably go to pot. The 22 type is a perfectionist with inclinations to martyrdom.

23. This number is the mark of someone who is dogmatic and possesses a rationalist mentality. The less kind would say that he or she is a "reductionist" because the viewpoint may be too narrow and not take into account any spiritual values whatsoever. As well as a stubborn adherence to materialism this person hates to be contradicted.

24.   This is an adventurous number denoting someone daring, far sighted and determined to experience life to the full. To those influenced by 24, life is a journey into the unknown, something to be embraced, with lots of stop off points along the way. This person will learn a lot, have many romances and be charmingly unconventional.

25.   This number is the mark of someone who is perceptive and intelligent with an open mind and a fertile imagination. This person is something of a visionary, who can see past the obvious and who is willing to allow his intuition to enliven the mental processes. Creativity is also evident in this number. Perhaps there is also a hint of genius.

26.   This number is the mark of a doer rather than a thinker. He is a person of action who cannot abide those who delay or make excuses. Friends and colleagues agree that the 26 type person is a useful member of any team. This number may also indicate someone whose job, though not generally glamorous, is absolutely necessary.

27.   A person who has 27 as one of the fate numbers does not lack courage. This is an indicator of heroism and fortitude. Of course any hero would be wasted without a cause to fight for so possessing this number is not usually an indicator of an easy or quiet life. If no cause is to be found this person will joyfully create his own personal crusade.

28.   Romance is the keynote for the 28 type person, who is never happy unless overwhelmed by passionate enchantment. It may be that such a person is not the ideal lover one would think because he is more in love with the concept of love than with

any particular person. Nevertheless the intensity of this person's emotion will sweep a lover off their feet.

29.　　There is no doubt that a person with 29 as a fate number has got distinct views and opinions and will not by shy in sharing them with all and sundry. Often, people of this type are constant letter writers. Some may take this gift and become newspaper columnists, authors or broadcasters. This is a person with iron convictions and a readiness to speak up.

30.　　Fame, popularity and a tendency to court public opinion are all factors affecting those with 30 as a fate number. In fact 30 type people may have prominence thrust upon them rather than actively seeking it out. There may also be an element of fickleness here as serial relationships and several weddings are not unlikely.

31.　　The hard working 31 type will not accept second best in anything. This person may not give himself the credit he deserves for his diligent efforts but demands that others respect his drive and ambition. This is another number that hints at the achievement of fame, though in this case prominence will have been hard won.

32.　　Partnerships of all kinds are emphasized by 32. Although a long lasting emotional link is by far the most important, business partnerships are also vital for the well-being of a 32 type person. This is because the happiness and progress of the significant other is as important to this person as his or her own happiness. This is a loyal and loving individual.

33.　　Early isolation will lead to an imaginative and creative nature. There is a sense of purity and other-worldliness about this number but there is also a vague feeling of unease or fearfulness that is difficult to put into words. Dreamy and impractical, it may be his deep spirituality that leads a 33 type person into the caring professions.

34. Anxiety is the main problem with 34 as a fate number. This unfortunate person has a mind that races in a million directions at once and will rarely give him any peace at all. Problems will constantly be blown out of proportion and the resultant neurosis can have a troubling effect on the health. Stress management is vital to this type.

35. This type of person is one who likes peace and harmony, however if such a blissful state does not exist, he will move heaven and earth to ensure that a temperate atmosphere will once again reign. Balance is vital to this person's psychological well-being. Many will take up vigorous exercise to attain the body beautiful too.

36. A person with 36 as a fate number is going to be very bright. In fact, in many cases the intelligence approaches genius level. Have no doubts, this person does not think on a small scale. Vast conceptions and the determination and energy to bring them to fruition are also traits of this number.

37. This is a pretty conventional number with happiness, domestic bliss and marital harmony foretold. A person with the number 37 as one of the numbers of fate likes order in his life. Not for him the life of a high flying socialite or an adventurer, just good old fashioned normality and relationship contentment are on offer with 37.

38.   It is rare that anything or indeed anybody comes up to a 38 type person's high expectations. In fact disappointments are a recurring feature for this type simply because he is likely to want too much from life. This is made worse by the capacity for envy.

39.   This person will certainly deserve praise by the bucketful. A 39 type person is likely to achieve something great. It may be an invention, a personal triumph that brings him to the attention of the public and the powers that be, or a discovery that revolutionizes life. Credit where credit is due, the applause should echo!

40.   Shock and scandal are the hallmarks of the fate number 40. A person who is influenced by this number may rise to a high position in society only to have this comfortable ivory tower rocked by controversy. The resulting furor may not exactly bring him down, but never again will the aura of notoriety be quite absent.

41.   Although the initial fortunes of this number are good there is a sting in the tail with 41. The possessor of this fate number is likely to make unwise associations with others. The trouble is that he will rarely understand himself enough to avoid such mistakes.

42.   Despite the modern assertion that 42 is the answer to "life, the universe and everything", the traditional interpretation of this number is pretty morbid and doom laden. As a fate number, 42 shows a person with a gloomy cast of mind. A positive attitude must be sought, and then things will improve greatly.

43. The quest for meaning is important to someone with 43 present among the numbers of fate. For some this search will take a conventional form as an interest in scientific or religious issues. However this is not necessarily so, others will seek meaning in a wide variety or other, less usual pathways. However it manifests, the curiosity of this person is eternal.

44. The main associations with the number 44 are those of power, of splendid surroundings, of pomp, glamour and a high public profile. In the past this number was associated with royalty, however today its symbolism is equally true of anyone who achieves fame. As a fate number 44 denotes a very high flyer indeed.

45. This number shows that this person is in tune with the ethics, values and desires of people in his own society. It could be said that he has "the common touch", and will rarely find himself ill at ease or unable to cope with those of a different background. He will do well in any profession that brings contact with the masses.

46. Fertility is the keyword for the number 46. One who is influenced by it is likely to have large a family and to cope with life in a practical manner. It also has a bearing on livestock and crops, which should thrive and prosper. In addition, the mind of this person is likely to be equally fertile and inventive, finding novel solutions to all problems.

47. This is a very fortunate number showing health, happiness and longevity. This person will live through several generations and he will have many happy years to look back on. Life may not always be exciting but for the most part it will be filled with contentment.

48. After all things are considered, 48 type people are excellent judges of character. Instinctively they can act like a courtroom with a legalistic mind to match. Although at first impression they will seem cool and calculating, once they have accepted you, you'll have no doubt that you have been carefully weighed up and the verdict is that you are worth knowing.

49. This number shows an acquisitive nature. This does not necessarily imply greed, but rather an insecurity that requires possessions, savings and a healthy investment scheme to make this person feel safe. Of course, then security becomes an obsession, because the greatest dread this person could feel is the danger of losing what he owns.

50. If this number is part of a person's fate, then there is no point in anyone trying to restrict him within a relationship or tie him down to a binding contract. Liberty is the watchword and he'll be prepared to fight for it. There is also the possibility of some form of imprisonment (not necessarily literally), but if so, then a pardon will be granted.

60. A parting from loved ones is likely when the number 60 is found in the List of Fates. Traditionally this number was said to be indicative of widowhood, however it is equally likely the some form of divorce or other sort of personal loss is revealed. This is a distressing number that teaches one how to cope with grief and to carry on.

70. A fortunate number, suggesting a keen intellect and good taste. This fate number denotes someone who is constantly evolving, one who may break away from his original environment and create something brand new. There is also an

indication of interest in scientific fields even though the essential nature is basically poetic.

75.   This number suggests wide horizons and a nature that will not be constrained by the restrictions of country, class or background. This is a true internationalist, more concerned with global issues than mere local concerns. Traditionally, the number 75 indicate a life filled with distant journeys.

80.   A person with this number in his fate will be anxious to provide a cure for the ills of the world. This may seem to be a tall order, yet this person will remain undaunted by the enormity of the task. In fact, opposition to this worthy desire will add fire and determination to the life's work. This is someone who gets things done!

81.   This is a number with magical associations. Traditionally, the number 81 revealed a magician in the Merlin or Gandalf mode. Even today, it can show someone who has more than one trick up his sleeve. It is also the mark of an expert in some obscure, difficult or specialized field. The only danger here is that this magician might bite off more than he can chew.

90.   This number returns to the less fortunate aspects of the root number 9. Selfishness is the main problem because a lack of concern for others will result in a lack of thought for the 90 type person. A refusal to recognize his or her own faults leads to "blind-spots" in the character, which in turn can cause rejection by others.

100. There is no doubt that someone with 100 as a significant factor in his or her fate is very lucky indeed. Traditionally

this number was said to show divine favor, and that its fortunate possessor was blessed. However it should be remembered that blessings come in many forms and some of them are not at all comfortable to live with.

120.   Patriotism is the watchword of this type. It could be said that a person with 120 as a fate number has a romantic attachment to his point of origin, his country and his heritage. However, this attachment may equally apply to a cause or philosophy and the unshakable conviction in the rightness of his arguments. Either way, he will gain a lot of praise and admiration.

200.   In common with most numbers with a base 2, the fate number 200 is fairly unfortunate. In this case it is indecisiveness that is the main problem. In fact this inability to make up the mind can be crippling as the person is swayed first one way and then the other. Until this vacillation is brought under control there will be little progress.

215.   To be blunt, this number is said to be difficult. However, the predicted calamity is not necessarily operative on a personal level, but it does hint that at some time in life the individual will be involved in a major crisis. The event may not directly involve the person himself, he may witness it instead.

300.   This number is indicative of a strong belief system and a faith that can withstand many temptations. As a fate number 300 shows a resolute character who will stand up for a point of principle. Religious and philosophical beliefs in particular are emphasized by 300, and a stunning conversion is likely at some time in life.

318.   This shows a person with a mission, someone with something of great importance to say, and one who will be absolutely determined to get his message across. In earlier times this fate number would have denoted a prophet or crusader, but today it is more likely to indicate someone involved in politics.

350.   Hope springs eternal for a person who is influenced by the number 350. No matter what trials and tribulations life throws at such a person he will always spring back ready to take on the world again. The 350 type is likely to be ready to fight for a cause. He or she is a crusader unwilling to allow injustice to win.

360.   A person with 360 as a fate number is likely to be home loving, with a strong, romantic attachment to his or her country and heritage. The troubles in society at large will be a cause of anxiety, but this does not imply a worrying do-gooder. On the contrary the 360 type person is more likely to be convivial and more optimistic that otherwise.

365.   An awareness of time, not merely in its normal day to day sense, but of the implications of eternity, is associated with this number. It may show someone who has a scientific inclination, or one who is fascinated by history, astronomy, astrology or indeed anything that transcends the era in which the person lives.

400.   A person influenced by the fate number 400 is likely to be a traveler; however the journey this person undertakes will be long and arduous. Of course this need not necessarily refer to a physical journey, it might equally mean a spiritual path.

Possibly paying off a karmic debt or embarking on a difficult quest for knowledge.

490.   A clever mind combined with a natural religious or philosophical sense ensures that the 490 type person is a seeker after truth. Many civilizations, peoples, faiths and belief systems will intrigue this person over the course of the years. Endless curiosity will lead this person to some startling conclusions about the purpose of human life.

500.   There is a strong sense of spirituality about a 500 type person. He will instinctively recognize meaning in the apparent jumble of universal events. For some this will take the form of conventional faith but others will seek a more individual path to enlightenment. The traditional significance of this number is "Holiness".

600.   Traditionally this number is said to one of perfection and those influenced by it are content only with the best of everything. This is not to imply that they are covetous but that only the most rare and tasteful objects will be allowed into their home, only the best education is acceptable for their children and so on.

666.   In keeping with its Biblical notoriety, the number 666 is bad news. It doesn't exactly mean that the possessor of this number is the Devil, just that he or she can act like one on occasions. This person makes a bad enemy and an unreliable friend. Much self awareness and work on changing attitudes will be needed.

700.   This number traditionally represents strength, fortitude and courage. It denotes a person who will not accept the possibil-

ity of defeat. He will accept challenges and win through. It also implies a stoical point of view, one that will weather both triumph and disaster, and as Rudyard Kipling said, "Treat those two impostors just the same".

800. The traditional significance of this number is "Empire" and those influenced by it will indeed be empire builders in one way or another. Seriously ambitious, this person will not allow anything to stand in his way, bucking the odds as he goes through life. This could be a Caesar, a politician, or a high-powered multinational executive in the making.

900. This number has a severely martial quality. It signifies wars, combats and struggles implying that 900 types are quarrelsome, competitive and willing to do anything to win. This aggressive drive may have its origins in childhood deprivations and this person will not cease until he has overcome all enemies and his inner demons.

1,000. A strong moral sense is revealed when the comparatively rare number 1,000 appears as part of the fate. However this morality is not harsh - quite the opposite in fact because its possessor is extremely compassionate, non-judgmental, forgiving, merciful and high minded. He may struggle to reconcile these ideals with harsh realities.

1,095. A person with this fate number is not the most forthcoming of individuals. Somewhat reclusive, this person may prefer his own company and will often resent the presence of others. This solitary trait often indicates mental preoccupation, the details of day to day existence merely providing a distraction to deep thought and philosophical abstractions.

1,260. This person will find it very difficult to forget bad experiences. This is more than a matter of possessing a good memory. There is a neurosis present here which tends to make life a struggle. This person constantly replays old events over and over in the mind and causes himself endless torment. Deep seated grief or guilt may be the root problem for this type.

1,300. The highest number in the List of Fates is also one of the most difficult to cope with. It signifies persecution and may reveal someone who suffers discrimination because of his beliefs, ethnic origins or political views. Nevertheless this person will courageously cling to the importance of the convictions come what may.

A Final Thought

While writing and updating the section on the List of Fates, Jonathan's next door neighbor Glenys asked if the system could be applied to house numbers. This had not occurred to either of us, so with some trepidation we tried it out, only to discover that apparently it did! So, if you live in a house or flat with a number, the List of Fates could possibly provide a guideline to what your fate will be while you are resident there. It also occurs to us that phone numbers might also provide another, hitherto ignored method of consulting the ancient List of Fates, especially in this age of mobile phones and the vast array of number combinations now in use.

If you have any useful experiences using such additional numbers, we would be interested in hearing about them, and you can contact us by email, at oracle@zampub.com. All correspondence will be kept strictly confidential.

The Mystic Pyramid

Like all the oracles in this book, the roots of this one are ancient. It was apparently popular in the middle ages and is said to have been used by that most famous of 18th century mystics, Cagliostro, to aid him in his divinations. A version of this was discovered early in the 19th century and translated from the Latin by a writer with the majestic pen name of "Grand Orient".

Jonathan has researched extensively the background to the system, so that we can understand what is behind it; although our discoveries are too esoteric and complex to put in a book of this size, we have taken the ideas from the original system and brought them bang up to date for you to use, without introducing unnecessary complexities.

How to use the Mystic Pyramid

The method is simplicity itself and the only equipment you will need, apart from this book, is a pendulum or a necklace with a pendant on it, or at a pinch a heavy needle dangling from a piece of cotton thread.

First, study the list of questions and pick the one that best fits what is on your mind.

Make a note of the question you wish to ask, including the letter of the alphabet beside your question, as this will help you to locate the answer.

Next, clear your mind and concentrate on your question; take your pendulum and dangle it over the Mystic Pyramid design, then allow this to drift around while you concentrate on your question. You can close your eyes while doing this if you like.

Now allow the pendulum to drop down and then make a note of the number it lands on (or closest to) on the Mystic Pyramid.

Once you have found the number in the Mystic Pyramid, search through the lists of answers in the next chapter, until you find the one that has your question at the top. The letter of the alphabet that is next to your chosen question will help you to locate this.

Then look through the 36 answers in the list until you find the one you picked from the Mystic Pyramid.

The Mystic Pyramid

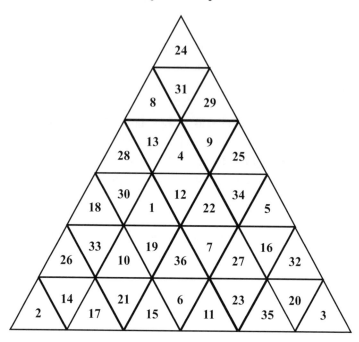

The list of questions

A   Will I find a meaningful love relationship?

B   Will my finances improve?

C   What is the potential for my career?

D   Will my family and home be happy?

E   Will my health improve?

F   Will this problem be resolved?

G   What will my luck be like in general terms?

Mystic Pyramid Lists of Answers

Look for your question (the letter of the alphabet should help you to locate this), then look down the list until you come to the number that you found in the Mystic Pyramid (in the previous chapter), and read the answer.

List A. Will I find a meaningful love relationship?

This is a straightforward question that can receive a yes, no or "it depends" type of answer. The Mystic Pyramid Oracle follows this with some necessary amplification about your present and future situation, and in some cases, useful advice about how to handle it.

1. Yes. The man you settle down with may not have much going for him in the looks department but he will certainly have money.

2. Yes. The person who you are now with is not likely to be part of your long-term future because there is a chance that you will end up with a previous lover who left and who will return. If neither of these options work out, someone new will come along.

3. Yes and no. You can certainly find lovers but you tend to attract unfaithful and disloyal ones, so choose carefully and

check them outthoroughly before making an irrevocable commitment.

4.   Yes. You can certainly find someone to love just as long as you don't set your sights too high.

5.   Yes. Your love life and also your status in life will soon improve.

6.   Yes. But, you have a tendency to attract abusive lovers so don't just jump at the first chance of a relationship that comes your way. Give the other person plenty of time to prove him or herself decent before making a firm commitment.

7.   Yes, and your lover will be truthful and true to you.

8.   Yes. A friend or lover who is travelling will soon return, and this could turn out to be the one for you.

9.   Yes. A loving partner and a large and prosperous family are indicated.

10.   Yes. You will marry a man who has very little money and you may never be rich, but with your help the two of you will get along very nicely and you will be happy together.

11.   Yes. You may meet someone while travelling or as a result of a journey.

12.   Not right now. Making money and getting ahead is more important for you at the moment than looking for a partner.

13. Yes. A letter will bring good news about love and this could lead to a permanent relationship.

14. Yes. But, you must take care about whom you trust. If you do, you will be fine, otherwise you could regret getting yourself involved.

15. Yes, but you will kiss plenty of frogs before you find your handsome prince or princess.

16. Yes. You will become involved with someone almost overnight, and despite the odds, this will turn out to be the one who stands the test of time.

17. Yes. You will have a pleasant partner and you should have children if you want them.

18. Yes. Don't give up, there is definitely someone out there for you, although it may take time before he or she comes along.

19. Yes. You won't be lonely for long because you will soon meet the right person.

20. Yes. Your lover may not have much money but he or she will be very loving and affectionate.

21. Yes. You will soon meet someone and you will have a happy partnership.

22. Yes and no. You could meet someone soon but you will need to guard against picking a drunk or some other waster and user. If you don't find the right person yet, leave it for a few months and try again later.

23.   Yes. You may already have found your lover but you may not know this yet.

24.   No. Friends and family are important to now, but all is not lost because love will come along later.

25.   Yes. Travelling could bring you luck and love, so don't sit around at home hoping that you handsome prince or lovely princess will jump out of the television at you, get out and meet people.

26.   Yes. But you must ensure that enemies don't take your lover away from you.

27.   Yes. You will be lucky without having to make an effort to find someone.

28.   Yes. Be patient, someone will come along quite soon.

29.   No. This doesn't mean that you will never find anybody, it is just that you are looking for love in all the wrong places right now and until you see what you are doing, nothing much will change.

30.   Yes. An affectionate and loyal lover will come along sooner or later.

31.   No. The problem is that you may be too fussy for your own good which is making it difficult for you to find someone who comes up to the impossible standards that you demand. There are good people out there as long as you learn not to ask for the moon.

32. Yes. You will suffer some setbacks and some potential relationships won't work out, but after a while you will find the one you want.

33. Yes. Don't worry, love will come your way. Relax and get on with other things until this happens.

34. No. You seem to be going after the wrong type or barking up the wrong tree. Perhaps you need to consider what you are doing that is holding you back from meeting nice people.

35. Yes. Tradition says that you will have a rich but jealous partner. If you need the money and can stand the jealousy, that's fine. Otherwise leave things for now and try the Mystic Pyramid Oracle again in a few months' time.

36. Yes. You will have a sober, steady, affectionate and decent lover, but he or she won't have much money.

List B. Will my finances improve?

This is a straightforward question that can receive a yes, no or "it depends" type of answer. The Mystic Pyramid Oracle follows this with some necessary amplification about your present and future situation, and in some cases, useful advice about how to handle it.

1. Yes. Your finances can be improved as long as you do not allow yourself to be swayed from your purpose.

2. Yes. You can improve your finances by getting on with important jobs while also remembering your obligations to others.

3. Yes. There is no doubt that luck is with you and that you will soon overcome your financial difficulties.

4. Not at the moment. You will suffer minor inconvenience or losses but these can be overcome in time.

5. Yes. Business opportunities are on their way. Make the most of them.

6. Yes. You will soon receive a rise in pay.

7. Not if you take chances. This is not a good time for speculative ventures but if you steer a steady course you should be all right. Keep your spending under control.

8. Depends. If you are in business, there is a calm quiet period ahead which may be useful for clearing up those jobs that you have been meaning to get around to, but it is not much good for money-making schemes. If you have a job, then

stay where you are and wait for better times to come along before you ask for a raise. Keep debts under control.

9.   Yes. You will soon have a sudden financial improvement. You may receive a legacy, a tax rebate or some other kind of windfall shortly.

10.   Yes. Your fortunes will soon change for the better.

11.   Depends. You are too ambitious at the moment and you may be aiming too high too soon. Take things easy for a while.

12.   Yes. You must plan properly and be clever in pursuing your plans. Be cunning if necessary but not disloyal or underhand.

13.   No. Something is coming to a complete end and disappointment or losses are likely. Keep some money back for the stormy times that are coming to you.

14.   Yes. If you avoid confrontations and quarrels, you will soon overcome your difficulties.

15.   Yes. Self-reliance is the key to success at the moment and you must avoid trusting others or relying upon them too much. Use your intuition, because if it tells you that the time is not right for something or that someone is not right for you to deal with, then back off.

16.   No. Keep your head down below the parapet. Avoid gossip and scandals and take care that you don't do anything that could rebound on you later on. Be prudent.

17. Yes. But you must keep your hard won funds for yourself and you should not lend money to others. If you lend money in the hopes of getting interest on your loan you will be disappointed.

18. Yes. You will soon overcome danger and be granted a long period of good fortune.

19. Yes. But, you must get out and about because opportunities for travel in connection with business or work will bring good fortune.

20. No. Not only are your finances poor at the moment but your health doesn't look good either. Look after yourself, don't overspend and wait for better times to come.

21. Yes. You may receive a wonderful surprise or a windfall soon.

22. Yes. However, you will only reach success after a prolonged period of effort.

23. Yes. As long as you are loyal and trustworthy and you keep away from dodgy dealings and other forms of deceit.

24. Yes. Be patient and plan carefully, because your future actions require careful thought.

25. No. Family problems will hold you back in business or in your career. Wait for better times to come and save what money you can in the meantime.

26.   Yes. You will soon have financial success and you will then invest your funds wisely.

27.   Yes. As long as you keep your promises to others, at work and in general life. Don't say one thing and then do something else.

28.   Yes. There should be a pleasant financial surprise coming along soon.

29.   No. You have many difficulties to face in the immediate future. Guard against unnecessary spending and wait for better times to come along.

30.   Not necessarily. However, your social life is about to improve and that may allow you to make contacts that could be useful for you in business or for finding the right kind of work in the future.

31.   Yes. Networking is the key to success for you, so keep in touch with old friends, as they may be able to do you a bit of good.

32.   Yes. You may win something through a competition. Also a partnership or relationship of some kind may benefit you financially.

33.   Yes. Big changes are afoot that will alter your surrounding circumstances in a way that works to your benefit.

34.   Yes. The near future will be extremely stressful but ultimately lucky. Keep at it and don't give up however rough it gets.

35.　No. Your money worries seem set to continue. Don't spend unnecessarily and wait for better times before committing yourself to anything.

36.　Depends. The problem is that your health is not wonderful at the moment and you are unlikely to have much strength to spare in the near future. Work as hard as you are able without making yourself ill and wait for better times before making unnecessary expenditure.

List C. What is the potential for my career?

Unlike lists A and B, this one cannot be answered in a straightforward "yes, no, depends" form, but the Mystic Pyramid Oracle gives you an idea of the future and in many cases, advice as to how best to achieve your goals.

1. Self-motivation is the answer. Nobody is about to help you at the moment and anything good that comes will only do so as a result of your own efforts.

2. Teamwork is the answer. The potential looks good as long as you are prepared to be a good team worker, so fit in with the plans of others as best you can and work for the benefit of the group as a whole.

3. Put your shoulder to the wheel because it is your own hard work and achievements that will get you anywhere. You can't sit back and let others do the work at this time.

4. Be realistic. Don't allow your dreams of success to reach beyond what is possible, on the other hand don't give up at the first hurdle. A proper and realistic analysis of your chances will give you the right idea.

5. Communicating with others is the name of the game for you. If this means looking for a job or looking out for improved prospects, talk to others, listen to what they have to say and keep your eyes open for opportunities.

6. Your career seems to be on hold at the moment and you may be better served by taking a spell away from work, looking after the family, having a rest and putting things right in other

areas of your life; or, if this is not possible, just marking time at your job for a while.

7.   You can make progress now if you use all your skills wisely. If there is something that you are trained for or experienced in that you can offer others, this is the time to do so. Also, sales and marketing may be the answer in some guise or another, even if it is only to make you more appealing to an employer.

8.   If you wish to open a business or to improve one, this is the time to get going. You will need courage and a touch of the gambler's instinct.

9.   Sales, marketing, cracking on with something and making things happen is the name of the game for you now. You either have to market yourself and your skills or some product or service that you are involved with.

10.   Your career prospects will succeed if you have faith in your abilities and self-confidence, and this will still work if you are wobbly inside but you make the effort to look confident. Make careful plans and they will turn out to be a success.

11.   Your work environment is so filled with hidden dangers, discord, trials and tribulations, treachery and struggles that it isn't worth making any more effort than is strictly necessary. You need to consider a change of job, a complete change of career, a break from work or even to go back into full time study and ultimately to do something completely different. The fact is that you won't go any further in your present job and you may even find yourself going backwards.

12.   You may overcome your present problems in time but you have some harsh lessons to learn before doing so. There seems to be intrigue, backstabbing and politicking going on around you and it may be you who ends up being sacrificed on the altar of someone else's ego. If the pressure gets worse, change your job before you get ill.

13.   You can get somewhere as long as you avoid throwing your weight about. If you use power unwisely, it will only bring destruction.

14.   Your chances of promotion are finely balanced, because on the one hand you could find yourself moved sideways or even right out of a job due to forces that are beyond your control, while on the other hand if you are careful and wise you will be able to hang in three. Put some savings by in case things don't work out.

15.   Your promotion prospects may be hampered by strange situations that may be of your own making or due to the actions of others. Greed, lust for power or even something sexual may be going on in your workplace. Someone around you lacks scruples and morals and he or she will go to any length to achieve their aims.

16.   Promotion is extremely unlikely in your present circumstances. Accidents, health problems and defeat by a hidden or open enemy are possible in the near future. Consider a new line of work, a new job or even a break from work.

17.   You can expect promotion after a period of difficulty. Keep to the straight and narrow and ask your spiritual guides or guardian angel for help if needs be.

18. The atmosphere around you at work is fraught with quarrels and danger. It doesn't look as though your present situation is likely to take you very far.

19. Promotion, happiness, esteem, success and honor are on the way to you now.

20. You may have to stop and think for a while because new plans are underway which may be the cause of a delay to your progress. It seems that your employers are looking for a new purpose, a new enterprise or new financing and this must happen before you can expect any real improvement.

21. Promotion is definitely on the way, along with advancement, honors, victory and success.

22. You must seek clarity both by being clear in your mind as to your true position and also by getting others to be open, honest and clear in their intentions towards you. You may find yourself being hampered by jobs that go wrong due to the bad judgement others or even from your own delusions and muddles.

23. You will soon receive help, protection and the favor of those who are in authority.

24. Promotion, good fortune, a rise in status and increased income are on the way to you now.

25. You will advance in your career as a result of the wisdom and strength that you gain through experience.

26. Guard against backing the wrong faction at your workplace or of trusting false friends or of taking advice that is ultimately harmful to you. Use your intuition, keep your eyes open and your mouth shut.

27. You will either shortly be helped by those who are in powerful positions or you yourself will soon be in one. Your mind is productive and you can make use of your intellect.

28. Guard against trusting the wrong people or believing all that you are told. Your fortunes will fluctuate and you may take a few steps forwards and backwards before your future becomes completely clear.

29. This job is too vague and uncertain for you to base a future upon. There seems to be deception around, trouble on the way and the chances are that the situation will get you down and even make you ill if you stick with it.

30. You can work your way upward by using your eyes and brain to work out what is going on in your place of work. If you happen to do brainwork in your job, you will go far.

31. You may need to tread a lonely road for a while, trusting nobody and holding to your own principles and judgement against the prevailing atmosphere which seems to be wrong for you.

32. You must hang on to your own values and principles even if they clash with those of others. However, you will also need to be extremely diplomatic because others will be stubborn and confrontational. If you can do this, you will ultimately ride out the storm and get somewhere with this job.

33.   Good fortune is on the way and this should help your promotion prospects.

34.   You are learning and gaining strength through experience and this will help you to reach the position that you desire.

35.   Don't take risks, don't trust the wrong person. Your so-called friends will let you down and any advice you receive now is useless or even positively harmful. Wait until better times come before going for promotion.

36.   You will soon reach the position that you most want.

List D. Will my family and home be happy?

Although this looks as though a straightforward yes/no answer can be given, it can't really, as so many of the answers depend upon the way you and others behave in the future.

1. There will soon be luck and prosperity for you and yours. Your family will increase in size, either because you decide to have more children, or through marriages, alliances and other connections.

2. Peace will reign in your home as long as everybody abides by the law and doesn't do anything stupid.

3. Friends may be more useful to you in the near future than your family is likely to be.

4. Your partner will be very loving and you will have no shortage of money, but you are unlikely to have many children or relatives.

5. The family is fine but your financial position will be difficult for a while. Hang on to what you have and be frugal until things improve.

6. Jealousy could wreck your relationship and split your family.

7. Family life looks good but your financial outlook is poor. Don't spend money on anything other than necessities for the time being.

8. Your partner will be terrific and he or she will be nice looking, pleasant, youthful and not short of ready money either.

9. You need to change your outlook and your behavior in order to make your family and your partner happy, then all will be well.

10. Take care that those with whom you mix don't bring you down and your family's reputation along with you.

11. You will have a large family and you will seek to educate your children well. This will bring honor to you and to the rest of your family.

12. Even though times may be hard at the moment, they will improve and the whole family will benefit as a result.

13. Secret enemies may try to harm or upset members of your family. Be on guard against them and you will win out in the end.

14. If you do the right thing by your family, they will appreciate this and love you in return. Even the few hard times won't leave a bad feeling, as the good ones will be more numerous.

15. You may not be able to make a family of your own if you remain fussy and unapproachable.

16. You and your family will travel in Europe on business and for pleasure and this will bring you luck and success.

17. Your marriage may not be all that good but your children will be a comfort to you.

18. You and your family will be happy and successful.

19.   After a few setbacks, you and your family will be happy and comfortable.

20.   Do the right thing, conduct yourself well, and you and your family will be happy and prosperous.

21.   You may have a difficult first marriage but it looks as though a second one and a subsequent family group will be much more successful for you.

22.   You will have many admirers but when you choose the right one, your home and family will be happy.

23.   Your partner seems to be running into difficulties at work or with money. Support him as best you can through this difficult time.

24.   A letter will come that announces the loss of money or some kind of unexpected expense. Otherwise things seem to be all right at home.

25.   A secret enemy may try to upset you or other members of your family. Take care not to allow this person to get away with it.

26.   Laziness - either yours or your partner's will cause your family loss and distress.

27.   You will have a wealthy partner but he or she may not put you first or pay enough attention to you. You may find yourself living with a workaholic.

28.   You don't seem to be very lucky as regards family life at the moment and it doesn't look as though you will have more than one child. Perhaps this is just as well if things are going to be this difficult.

29.   Your lover is sincere and your family is loving and happy.

30.   You could choose the wrong partner, perhaps one who is too old for you and something of a misery. Think before getting into anything as it could make you and your family unhappy.

31.   Be cautious about who you choose to make your life with. Fortunately, there will be plenty of offers. If you are already with the wrong person, it will take time for this to be sorted out.

32.   Don't push your luck, don't try to dominate or bully your partner, your family or your children or you will lose them.

33.   Your partner appears to be deceptive and unreliable and this will affect the whole family.

34.   If you get into difficulties, turn to friends rather than family as they will advise and help you.

35.   Don't throw your heart and your family life away on a lover who is a waste of time.

36.   If you rush into marriage, you will be very disappointed, if you wait for the right person and the right time, you will have a happy family.

List E. Will my health improve?

This one poses a straightforward question, which can be answered by a yes, no or "it depends" type of answer in most cases, along with the usual amplification and occasional pieces of advice.

1. Yes. Your health will improve, and even more so when you take yourself in hand and make the necessary adjustments in your lifestyle.

2. Eventually. But you will have to look behind what is causing your sickness to see if there is any underlying cause or stress element can be tackled.

3. Yes. You will soon be feeling on top of the world.

4. Yes. Your health and strength will soon return.

5. Yes. But you may need to find the right doctor or advisor before you see any real improvement.

6. Yes. You will soon be feeling happier and healthier. As your love life improves, so will your health.

7. Yes. But you may have to take steps to find the right healer or doctor before you can see any real improvement.

8. Yes. Your health will get back into balance again, although you might benefit from some kind of alternative therapy in order to bring this about.

9. Eventually. But you will be stuck at home or stuck in your situation for some time. See what you can learn from this and how you can improve things for yourself.

10.   Yes. You are definitely on the up and up and as everything else in your life starts to improve, so will your health.

11.   Yes. You will soon be fully fit once again.

12.   Eventually. It will be some time before you feel better and you may have to take some fairly drastic steps to bring this about.

13.   Eventually. Your present situation is about to change in a dramatic way. If an operation or some other drastic treatment is needed, you will have to go for it.

14.   Yes. You will soon get your body and mind back into balance and you will feel at peace.

15.   Depends. If you are truly sick, it will be a while before you are well again but if it is your mental or emotional state that is making you ill, you will have to break these chains first before your health can hope to improve.

16.   Depends. There is some kind of underlying condition that must be brought out into the open and treated. You may not even be fully aware of this yet.

17.   Yes. There is every hope for the future and you should soon be fully recovered.

18.   Not yet. There seems to be an underlying condition that is not helping your health situation. This may be a medical condition or it may be worry and unhappiness that is holding you back from full recovery.

19.   Yes. You will soon be fit and bursting with energy.

20.   Not yet. You can't go on as you are, something has to change. You may need to change your lifestyle, your eating habits or something else before your health can hope to improve.

21.   Yes. You will soon be fine once again.

22.   Depends. A new treatment, a new outlook, a new lifestyle may be what is needed. You can't go on in the same old way and also expect to feel well.

23.   Yes. You will soon be in a position to do something about your health situation. This may require fairly drastic action.

24.   Yes. Finding the right doctor, therapist or advisor will give you the answer to your health problems.

25.   Eventually. You must read up about your condition and find out all you can about putting it right.

26.   Eventually. Once other aspects of your life improve, your health will too. You probably need a rest more than anything else.

27.   Depends. Your health is not good and it will take time before you either find a way of dealing with it or living with it as best you can.

28.   Depends. A new outlook is needed and perhaps some new kind of treatment.

29.   Depends. Life is not easy right now and there is too much for
        you to handle. Perhaps it is this that is making you ill.

30.   Yes. You will soon feel better and your life will be less re-
        stricted.

31.   Yes. Your health is definitely improving, although you will
        still worry about this from time to time.

32.   Yes. You will soon be feeling very well and you will put the
        health problem behind you.

33.   Yes. You need small treatments, possibly a bit of pampering
        or alternative therapies because there is not much that is
        needed to put you right.

34.   Depends. You may need to take some fairly drastic action to
        improve your health. Getting away from your environment
        for a while might help.

35.   Eventually. Take advice from your women friends, as they
        will know more about your condition than you do, and they
        could help you.

36.   Eventually. Seek out professional help and advice and once
        you have found a doctor or therapist you can trust, do what
        they tell you to do.

List F. Will this problem be resolved?

Whereas the five previous questions have been pretty specific, this one relates to a problem that could affect any part of your life. The answers might need a bit of thinking about before you see what can or should be done if anything.

1. You will have to work very hard for very little in return for a while and it will be some time before you find answers to your problems.

2. Others around you may have money and if your problem is financial, they could help you, but this is accompanied by so much criticism that it hardly feels worth letting them do so.

3. You seem to have a rival and even if it doesn't look like it on the face of things, jealousy is likely to harm you. As long as you keep your eyes open, things should work out reasonably well.

4. If your problem is one that loosely comes under the umbrella of creativity it will be fine, but if it is financial, things don't look so good.

5. Don't sit about worrying about things, do something!

6. Don't surround yourself by useless or addictive people. Choose your friends and colleagues wisely and all will be well.

7. Be honest and industrious and you will triumph over your enemies and your problems.

8.   Educate yourself and those around you because knowledge will give you the answer to this problem.

9.   Your problems look like getting worse rather than better. Don't rely upon others because they will let you down.

10.   You will have luck in relationship matters and other things should be fine too.

11.   You seem to be surrounded by some really awful people and your problems won't be solved until you move on and leave them behind you.

12.   If your problem is related to love, then it can't be solved other than by splitting up and calling it a day. Otherwise, things will be reasonable as long as you avoid envious people.

13.   Travel and movement seem to be the answer to your problem.

14.   It will take you time before you can find the allies and even the lover that you want or to sort out other types of problem.

15.   A secret enemy seems to be looking for ways of hurting you. Whether this is the cause of your present troubles or not, it is worth knowing that all is not as it seems.

16.   Nothing good will come of this situation, you must make a complete change before things improve.

17.   Be careful with whom you get involved, as bad company could make your problems worse rather than better.

18. If your problem means that you have to deal with another person, bear in mind that this person is deceitful.

19. Go your own way, because others can only make this problem worse. Rely upon yourself, you will sort things out.

20. Yes, your problem will soon be solved and you will be happy once again.

21. The needs and desires of others are not actually your problem, so you must concentrate on what is best for you.

22. You may be short of money, love or something else that you want but this situation will soon change for the better.

23. You seem to be the architect of your own downfall. Don't try to deceive others and try to control the more woolly headed side of your nature if you wish to solve your problems.

24. Flattery will make you swelled headed but it won't solve your problems.

25. It will take time for this problem to be solved and there may even be a few more on the way before you can see clearly what is going on and what you should do about them.

26. If yours is a love problem, you are probably better off without the person who is responsible for it. If the problem is not related to love, things will be fine as long as you don't allow others to lead you up the garden path.

27. Those around you may look good but they are deceitful. Rely on yourself to solve your own problems.

28.   Wealth, happiness and peace of mind are on the way to you.

29.   If you are in need of a lover or a business partner, this is on the way. Other problems will soon solve themselves but you can find good advice if you need it.

30.   Friends and family may be the key that opens the door to a solution to your problems. They may be able to do something practical to help you or they may help by simply being there to listen and talk.

31.   Your friends are sincere but they may advice you to take short cuts when you need to take a longer view of things.

32.   You will soon solve your problem but you will be sad because a dear friend will move out of your orbit.

33.   You can't allow others to push you in a direction that is wrong for you, so ultimately you will solve your own problems in your own way.

34.   Try to solve the problems you have in a sensible way and not by taking chances or by trusting the wrong people.

35.   Good fortune and happiness are coming your way, but if a member of the opposite sex is responsible for your problem they will continue to be troublesome.

36.   Business and money will improve, your love life will be reasonable and all other problems will fade away before long.

List G. What will my luck be like in general terms?

This is obviously a rather vague question so the answers may or may not be straight to the point. You will have to think carefully about what the Mystic Pyramid Oracle tells you, as it might apply to your present situation or to events in the more distant future.

1. Your luck will be fine as long as you stick to what you are doing now and don't allow others to sway you from your purpose. Tune in to your ambitions and aim high for success.

2. As long as you do not neglect important duties and obligations, things will be fine.

3. You will overcome difficulties and achieve happiness in the end. If you need help, pray to whichever deity you believe in.

4. You will suffer minor inconveniences and a loss in the short term but you will get over these after a while. You will soon have power, wisdom and stability.

5. Business opportunities will come your way and you are advised to make the most of them. Your marriage or partnership will be happy.

6. Your love life will be fine and someone who cares about you will give you a nice present. You can also expect a rise in pay due to doing a job well.

7. Don't take chances or gamble on anything right now as Lady Luck is not with you at the present time, but your general life trends are rather good.

8.   There is a period of peace and calm ahead. Enjoy this and don't worry about it, as it won't be long before you are busy again. If you need justice or a balance in your life you will get this.

9.   You will be lucky due to a sudden financial gain, but something in your personal life will give you a certain amount of grief.

10.   The wheel of fortune is turning your way at last and lucky breaks are all around you. Your self-confidence will return, your plans will work out, and you will have honor heaped upon you. Have faith.

11.   Your plans may be too ambitious and you may be aiming too high too soon. Hidden dangers and even treachery may be around you.

12.   Your health may suffer due to sacrificing too much of your time and energy for the benefit of others. A visit to a town or city will prove lucky.

13.   You will soon be in a position of power, which you must use in the right way, because if you use it wrongly you will bring destruction down on yourself and others. A disappointment or loss is likely.

14.   Be careful where you go and keep your wits about you because you may find yourself in a dangerous situation, but your luck as far as business and money are concerned will be rather good. Avoid confrontations and quarrels and you will overcome your difficulties.

15. On one hand, the fates are telling you to guard against letting your desire or lust for someone or something overtake you because it could land you in trouble. However, if the person you fancy is free to love and willing to do so, you are in for a very passionate phase indeed.

16. Take care when dealing with sharp tools or fire because accidents are possible. However, your love life will be spectacularly good and perhaps you will be in such a dazed state by this that you forget to concentrate when doing dangerous jobs.

17. You will overcome your present difficulties and you might be conscious of help from a guardian angel. Do not lend money at this time because you will end up losing your money and your friendship.

18. There will be bitter quarrels, probably over money, property or resources of some kind in the short term, but overall you can expect a long period of good fortune.

19. Happiness, esteem, honor and success are on the way to you. Opportunities for travel will bring good fortune.

20. You will soon have a new purpose, new plans and things to do, but like all new ventures there will be a few setbacks and delays. You must take better care of your health.

21. Advancement, honors, victory and a rise in status are on the way and a superb surprise awaits you.

22. You will reach success after a prolonged period of effort but you must keep your feet on the ground and be realistic.

23. Expect help, protection and the favor of those who are in positions of authority. Be loyal to those who deserve your loyalty, don't be tempted into bad behavior, and all will be well.

24. You can expect love, good fortune and a rise in status but you must be patient and give careful thought to all your actions.

25. Wisdom and strength can be gained as a result of experience but you can also expect a few family problems.

26. Avoid unwise speculations and don't trust the advice of friends as it may not be to your advantage, but wise investment brings financial success.

27. You will soon be in a position of authority and able to command others. Your intellect will be turned up high and your ideas will produce results. Be sure to keep your promises to others.

28. Don't be too trusting and don't expect things to keep on going well because there will be some setbacks, but there will also be high spots to enjoy. A surprise offer will please you.

29. An important letter is on the way to you. You can expect some uncertainty and even deception and you may work yourself up into a state of anxiety over this.

30. Your mind will be extremely acute and you will work out what needs to be done by a process of thought and deduction. Some nice things like a wedding or some other kind of

celebration may be in the air and there will certainly be pleasant social gatherings and parties to look forward to.

31. Even when others try to persuade you to do things that you know are not right, you will adhere to your principles, and while this may make you feel like an outsider for a while, you won't mind this too much. Expect a meeting with an old friend.

32. Marriage or partnership is in the air now. You will need to use diplomacy while sticking to your guns despite the stubborn opposition of others. Luck in competitions and relationships is to be expected.

33. Pure love and good luck are on the way to you now. Big changes are afoot that will be to your benefit.

34. You will become wise through experience and although you will go through some hard times, this will only make you stronger. The next week or two will be stressful but ultimately lucky. This could be a turning point.

35. Health and harmony are on the way now, but you must avoid trusting what others say too much. You may also have a few money worries. Use your intuition when dealing with others.

36. You will soon have some very bright ideas that can lead on to success. You will soon be in a position of power and authority but you must remember to take care of your health.

Index

Chinese Divinations

"A unique Compendium of Chinese Divinations..."

Sasha Fenton wanted to see if it is possible to produce
one book, containing the basics of many different Chinese
Divinations - and she more than achieved her aim!

This book goes much further than just the basics, but it
proves that Westerners can use and understand Chinese
systems with ease.

Contents include:

Face Reading	Feng Shui
Mah Jong Reading	Chinese Hand Reading
The Four Pillars of Destiny	Nine Star Ki (The Lo Shu)
Weighing the Bones	Yarrow Stick Reading

and a Chinese Lunar Oracle.

Paperback
240 pages

ISBN 0-9533478-5-0
£9.99

Astrology... on the Move!

"Where on Earth should you be?"

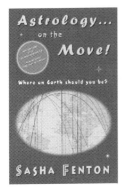

Sasha's book shows how any geographic location exerts a major influence on your life, and how a change of location can affect you, by way of a long-term move, or even simply choosing the right venue to ensure an enjoyable vacation.

Now in its 2nd. edition, revised & updated, there is also an exciting new section on astrological Feng Shui, to help you make the most of your home or business premises!

In her well-known, uncomplicated writing style, Sasha shows you how to use and understand three different, popular mapping techniques.
You don't have to be an astrologer to use and understand geographic astrology. Few other books exist on the subject; none are as accessible as this one.

"This book will help you to understand better where you have been, are now, and are going in the future." Roy Gillett, President, Astrological Association of Great Britain

Paperback   ISBN 0-9533478-0-X
190 pages   £9.99

Prophecy for Profit

"The essential Career & Business Guide for those who give Readings"

Sasha Fenton and her husband Jan Budkowski combine decades of divinatory & financial skills in this internationally oriented book.

Subjects covered include:
Organisational methods... A mental & physical health guide... Starting-up costs... Building up your clientele... Managing finance & cash-flow... Working in fairs & festivals... The Marine Bandsman Syndrome... Psychic protection... Teaching & Lecturing... and much more!

If you're serious about your career, this is the book for you - whatever your divination, from Astrology to Zoomancy!

"This book is a true gemstone. It should be on every Reader's MUST HAVE list, and should be recommended to anyone working part time or professionally, or indeed considering Reading as a vocation."
Andrew Smith, The Celtic Astrologer magazine

Paperback
240 pages

ISBN 0-9533478-1-8
£10.95

TEA CUP READING

"Tasseography... the art of reading Tea leaves & Coffee grounds"

Whatever your favorite brew, Sasha Fenton, international author of 24 books on various forms of divination, has written a practical guide for anyone who wants to use this particularly homely and easy-to-learn way of looking into the future - be it with Tea leaves or Coffee grounds!

Contents include:

cup preparation
techniques for reading tea cups
brief histories of Tea & Coffee
a dictionary of leaf & ground shapes
interpretation of the shapes
advice and tips

Paperback
138 pages

ISBN 0-9533478-3-4
£6.99

Fortune Telling by Tarot Cards

(Release date: Autumn 2001)

So far, this book has sold over 500,000 copies worldwide, confirming that Sasha Fenton's well-known, friendly & accessible style clearly sets a standard amongst the multitude of Tarot books available today.

Fully revised, updated and packed with fresh information for today's world, Sasha's popular title is once again available, and now illustrated throughout with the new Jonathan Dee Tarot deck!

This book is the ideal introduction to the Tarot.

Contents include:

Tarot origins   Intro to Major & Minor Arcana
Clear card interpretations   Linked / Synthesized card Readings
Simple, Complex & Special Purpose Readings
Volunteer Readings - and what happened later!

Paperback   ISBN 1-903065-18-6
about 180 pages   £8.99

For full details of other Zambezi Publishing books, forthcoming titles, and much more... visit our website at www.zampub.com

Forthcoming highlights include:

Quantum Perception
"Mind Power beyond the Senses"
by Zak Martin

This intriguing book offers a powerful intellectual argument for the existence of psychic powers and events, and the way they manifest themselves. Zak Martin, professional natural Psychic and past president of the Psychic Society of Ireland, presents this compelling assessment of psychic abilities today.

~~~~~~

The annual "Forecast" series
by Sasha Fenton & Jonathan Dee

Under the new series name: "Forecasts (2002,etc.)", **all twelve sun signs** are covered in one book, with weekly readings, Critical Event Days, Nutshells, monthly assessments for Love, Career, Money, Health & Luck, and much more!
Check our website or your favorite bookshop for up-to-date information,
and...
Latest news about our new **eBooks** and **DiskBooks** ™
All on **www.zampub.com** - have a look today!

~~~~~~

Trade info: Our UK and international distributors are listed on the website.